Hawks & Eagles

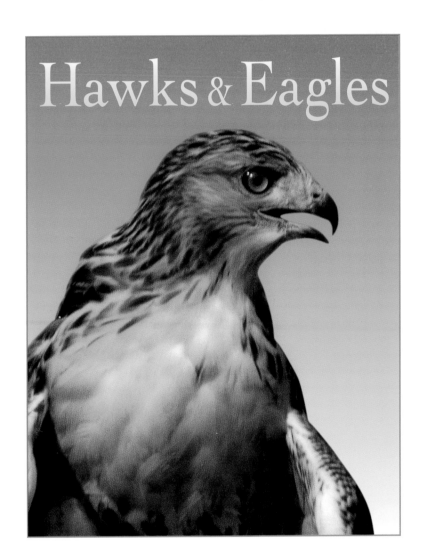

GEORGE K. PECK

SMART APPLE MEDIA

Published by

Smart Apple Media

123 South Broad Street

Mankato, Minnesota 56001

☙

Copyright © 1998 Smart Apple Media.

International copyrights reserved in all countries.

No part of this book may be reproduced in any form without

written permission from the publisher.

Printed in the United States of America.

Photos by George K. Peck,

Mark Peck,

Michael Sedor, Sid & Shirley Rucker / GeoImagery

Editorial assistance by Barbara Ciletti

Library of Congress Cataloging-in-Publication Data

Peck, George K.

Hawks & Eagles / written by George Peck.

p. cm.

Includes index.

Summary: Describes the physical characteristics, behaviors, and habitats of

several species of avian predators.

ISBN 1-887068-15-5

1. Hawks—North America—Juvenile literature.   2. Eagles—North

America—Juvenile literature. [1. Hawks. 2 Eagles.] I. Title.

QL696.F32P435   1998   96-19421

598.9'16—dc20   CIP

                                                                     AC

5 4 3 2

C O N T E N T S

W hen the founding fathers of the United States searched for an animal symbol to represent their new nation, they looked at many powerful and admirable beasts.

The animal they chose would become the national emblem of the United States of America. They had to choose carefully.

There was the majestic bison, master of the Great Plains. The ferocious Grizzly Bear, the country's largest predator. The proud American Elk with its colossal antlers. Even the deadly Diamondback Rattlesnake and the spectacularly feathered Wild Turkey were considered.

They wanted an animal as wild and as strong as their new country. A creature both fierce and independent. Both powerful and beautiful. A creature to inspire admiration, awe, and reverence.

They chose the Bald Eagle.

Eagles and hawks belong to the family Accipitridae, which also includes kites, harriers, and ospreys. There are 224 species in the Accipitridae family, all of them birds of prey, or raptors. They live on every continent except Antarctica and are found in a wide variety of habitats, from dry desert regions to towering mountains, from the steamy tropics to the chilly Arctic tundra. Twenty-five species are known to live and breed in the United States and Canada.

Hawks and eagles have learned to survive in nearly every habitat. The Rough-legged Hawk breeds in the Arctic tundra, while the Harris' Hawk prefers the hot southwestern deserts. The Snail Kite is found in Florida's hot, humid Everglades. The Northern Harrier lives and hunts in open fields. The fast-flying Sharp-shinned and Cooper's Hawks live in forested areas where their speed and agility help them capture woodland birds in midflight.

Bald Eagles are found across most of North America. The Bald Eagle is a fish-eating member of the Accipitridae family and is usually seen near open water. Its close relative, the Golden Eagle, prefers mountainous and inland regions. It is more common in the western half of North America.

Like the Bald Eagle, the Osprey is a fish-eater and is found near coastlines, rivers, and lakes around the world.

An Osprey near the shore of Sulton Island, Maine.

We usually think of hawks and eagles as large birds, but some of the smaller members of the family are only about the size of a robin. The tiny African Little Sparrow Hawk of South Africa measures less than 10 inches (25 cm) from head to tail. It weighs just 3 ounces (84 g) and has a wingspan of 15 1/2 inches (39 cm). The smallest North American hawk, the Sharp-shinned Hawk, is only about the size of a Blue Jay. But as a rule, hawks and eagles tend to be large. The biggest of all is the Harpy Eagle of Central and South America. It measures over 41 inches (104 cm) long, with a wingspan of nearly 6 1/2 feet (2 m). An adult female Harpy Eagle can weigh as much as 20 pounds (9 kg).

The Golden and Bald Eagles of North America are also quite large. A female Bald Eagle can have a longer wingspan than the Harpy Eagle's, but its body is smaller and lighter. As with most hawk and eagle species, the females are larger than the males.

Because hawks and eagles are predators, they are armed with strong legs and sharp, curved talons that help them kill and hold their prey. They have hooked beaks for tearing their food. At the base of their beak is an area of bare skin called the cere. The cere is sometimes brightly colored in shades of yellow and red.

Hawks and eagles hunt from the air. They rely on their eyes to locate prey, and they hunt only during the day.

Hawks and eagles can see four to eight times better than most humans. When you look up in the sky and see a high-flying hawk or eagle, you might not even be sure what kind of bird it is. But it can see you. If it could count, it could count the buttons on your shirt. A person who has very sharp vision might be called "eagle-eyed," but even the most sharp-sighted human can't see as well as a hawk or eagle. A hawk can spot the tiny movements of a feeding mouse from hundreds of yards in the air.

Eagles, ospreys, and the larger hawks known as Buteos have broad wings that help them catch warm air currents, lifting them high above the earth where they can soar for hours.

The five species of kites found in North America are smaller birds with long, pointed wings. The widespread Northern Harrier also has long wings, but with rounded tips.

The Accipiters, a group of small hawks that includes the Sharp-shinned Hawk and the Northern Goshawk, have short, rounded wings that help them chase other birds through the branches of their native woodlands.

9

Every hawk and eagle species has its own unique markings and colors. The adult Bald Eagle is the only eagle in North America with both a white head and white tail. The Red-tailed Hawk gets its name because its upper tail feathers are reddish-brown. No other North American member of the family has this particular mark. The Osprey is also easy to identify. This large bird is usually seen flying above water. It has a white head and belly, a dark brown stripe leading from the eye to the back, and each of its long wings has a dark patch on its underside.

But many hawks and eagles can be hard to tell apart. Sharp-shinned and Cooper's Hawks are almost identical, except that the Cooper's Hawk is larger and has a slightly longer tail. When a hawk is flying, or perched high in a tree, it's almost impossible to tell how big it is. When identifying hawks and eagles it is important to look at every detail, from the colors of the feathers to the shape of the wings and tails. Even the experts are sometimes fooled.

Young hawks and eagles are even more difficult to identify. Before they grow their adult plumage, the immature birds look more alike than ever. Immature Bald Eagles look like immature Golden Eagles. Their mottled and varied coloring makes them easy to confuse with large hawks, ospreys, and even vultures. The Bald Eagle does not get its distinctive white head and tail until it is four or five years old.

Bald Eagle landing on its perch in Alaska.

Hawks and eagles are mainly meat-eaters. They hunt other creatures, from insects to reptiles to small mammals. They hunt and kill with ease, often by surprise, coming out of nowhere to descend upon their prey. They are fast, quiet, and powerful hunters. Strong legs with sharp talons seize prey with such force that the victim dies immediately.

Some species have adapted to capturing certain types of prey.

Other species, such as the Osprey and the Bald Eagle, feed mainly on fish. The Osprey will spot a fish from high in the air and dive straight down into the water to capture it. It has spiny foot pads to help it grab and hold onto slippery fish. Bald Eagles will snatch fish from the surface of the water. They also feed on dead fish and animals.

The Snail Kite eats mainly apple snails, a large snail found in the Florida Everglades. Sharp-shinned and Cooper's Hawks eat small birds. They take their catch to a favorite "plucking post," where they pull off all its feathers before tearing it to bits and eating it.

While some hawks and eagles look for certain foods, many can and will adapt to whatever is available. The Red-tailed Hawk dines on everything from rabbits and mice to lizards, snakes, and crabs. The Mississippi Kite mostly eats insects such as grasshoppers, dragonflies, and beetles, but it will also eat frogs and small lizards. The American Swallow-tailed Kite has been known to eat everything from mice to insects to fruit!

Like other birds of prey, hawks and eagles when feeding will mantle, or cover, food with their wings in order to hide it from a hungry neighbor. These birds don't like to share territory, let alone dinner.

Different hawks and eagles are built for different styles of flying. The smaller hawks and kites are rapid, agile flyers. They need speed and quick reactions to catch their prey. Sharp-shinned and Cooper's Hawks have short, rounded wings that help them dart in and out of tree branches. The Northern Harrier takes off from low perches, flying low over fields and wetlands, ready to drop on its prey in an instant.

Eagles and the larger hawks are adapted to soaring. They hunt from high above the ground. These larger birds do not waste energy by flapping their wings when they don't have to. They seek out rising columns of warm air called thermals. They catch the rising air with their large, broad wings. The thermals carry them thousands of feet into the air in a slow spiral. You can watch a Bald Eagle soar for a very long time without ever seeing it flap a wing. Some migrating hawks and eagles use thermals during migration, coasting from one thermal to the next.

Most birds that breed in northern climates during the summer fly south for the winter. Any bird that needs fruit, fresh vegetation, or insects must travel south or they will starve. This twice-a-year journey is called migration.

Not all North American hawk and eagle species migrate. Because hawks and eagles are predators, they can survive the cold winter months. Some, like the Red-tailed Hawk and the Northern Goshawk, might fly a few hundred miles south during the winter if food is scarce, but they usually stay in the same region all year long. Many of the southern hawks and kites do not migrate at all. The Snail Kite, which eats a type of snail, never leaves Southern Florida. The Bald Eagle, a fish-eater, may travel south or to the coast to be near open water—but not always. Some eagles spend their winters in the northern United States, living on other types of prey.

Migrating hawks and kites include the Broad-winged Hawk, Swainson's Hawk, the Mississippi Kite, and the Swallow-tailed Kite. These birds all fly to South America for the winter. Swainson's Hawk is the champion migrator of the hawk and eagle clan—it flies all the way from western Canada to Argentina!

The courtship flight of the Bald Eagle is one of the most spectacular animal rituals in nature. The male and female eagles perform swooping dives, sometimes soaring together and then diving in a huge arc, down and then up again as if following the path of a giant, invisible pendulum. Sometimes the male eagle will dive down toward the female flying beneath him. Just before he reaches her, she will roll onto her back and the two great birds will clasp claws for a moment in midflight touching talons. Other hawks and eagles perform similar displays.

Most hawks and eagles mate for life. Smaller hawk species, such as the Sharp-shinned Hawk, may choose a mate when they are one year old. Larger hawks and eagles do not begin to breed until they are four or five years old. Some of the largest tropical eagles, such as the Harpy Eagle, may take as long as nine years to choose their mates.

Like most predators, hawks and eagles are extremely territorial. They don't like to share their food source with other birds of prey. During the breeding season, territory becomes more important than ever. Northern Goshawks and Swainson's Hawks have been known to attack human beings who wander too close to their nesting site.

Eagles may defend territories as large as 100 square miles (260 km^2). Smaller hawks may only need a territory the size of a few city blocks. Once hawks and eagles find a place to mate and raise a family, they may return year after year.

When human beings look for a new house, the first thing they want is a good location. Hawks and eagles also want to live in a good neighborhood. They want a home with a good view of their territory. They want to be near their food source. And they want to be safe from other predators.

When a pair of Bald Eagles search for a nesting site, they look for a location that will serve them for many years to come. Eagles need a big, sturdy tree or a rock ledge high on a cliff. Eagle nests are not your ordinary bird's nest. They don't just gather a few twigs and grasses and call it a nest. Eagles use branches and sticks, the bigger the better. They build a large, flat-topped nest large enough to hold you and several of your friends. Every year they return to the same nest and make it bigger. One famous Bald Eagle nest in Ohio sat 81 feet (25 m) above the ground in a hickory tree. It measured 8 1/2 feet (2.6 m) across, 12 feet (3.7 m) deep. It weighed about 2 tons (1,800 kg). After 35 years of use, the nest was destroyed in a windstorm.

Ospreys also reuse their nests, making them bigger every year. They like the same types of locations as the Bald Eagle, but have been known to build nests on electrical towers or telephone poles.

Of course, many nests are smaller. The Sharp-shinned Hawk builds a nest only 1 1/2 feet (45 cm) wide and 8 inches (20 cm) deep. The Northern Harrier nests on the ground, and the Snail Kite nests low in the Florida marshes, just a few feet above water.

Large eagles lay only one to three eggs, while the smaller hawks may lay three to five eggs. Eggs are laid two to five days apart. The eggs must be kept warm by the parents. This warming is called incubation. In most hawk and eagle species, both male and female take turns incubating. A few species, including Golden Eagles and Northern Goshawks, leave the incubation entirely to the mother. Incubation takes from four to nine weeks, depending on the size and type of bird.

The eggs hatch at different times. The first eggs laid are usually the first to hatch. Baby hawks and eagles come into the world wearing a layer of soft down that is later replaced by feathers. Their mother stays busy keeping each baby warm as it hatches from its shell.

While the mother stays with the nest, the father leaves to hunt for food. Growing hawks and eagles have big appetites. When the babies are older, the mother will sometimes leave them alone while she hunts for food too.

Baby hawks and eagles grow quickly. Smaller species such as the Sharp-shinned Hawk are fully feathered and ready to leave the nest in four weeks. Eagles and large hawks wait a little longer to take their first flight. Young Bald Eagles remain in their nest for 10 to 13 weeks.

The whole family stays together as the youngsters gain weight and develop into strong hunters and flyers. Even after they learn to hunt, they may still get some food from their parents. Young eagles may be fed by their parents for as long as a year.

Female Cooper's Hawk feeding a songbird to its young.

Hawks and eagles are fierce, powerful predators, but even the biggest and fastest creatures have enemies in nature. Hawk and eagle eggs can be stolen by raccoons and other tree-dwellers. Nestlings can be killed by other birds of prey. Small hawks are hunted by larger hawks. And when prey animals are in short supply, even the best hunters sometimes die from starvation. These are dangers that hawks and eagles have faced for millions of years.

In this century, however, the greatest danger to birds of every variety comes from people. Hawks and eagles are killed by landing on high-voltage power lines. Pesticides and pollution are especially harmful to the larger birds of prey. In the 1960s, an insecticide called DDT caused large hawks and eagles to lay eggs with shells so thin they crumbled. DDT poisoning became so bad that the Bald Eagle, the national symbol of the United States, was driven to the verge of extinction in the eastern part of the country.

In the past, hawks and eagles were commonly shot, poisoned, and trapped. Farmers, hunters, and ranchers believed that these birds hunted poultry, game birds, songbirds, and livestock. There are stories of eagles stealing sheep and other livestock, and even carrying off small children, but we know now that these stories are not true. A full grown eagle can lift only about 7 pounds (3.2 kg). It is true that a few domestic and game birds are taken by hawks, but hawks also do more good than harm by preying upon rats, mice, and insects that cause crop damage.

Loss of habitat and damage to the environment still threaten many hawk and eagle species. Some, such as the American Swallow-tailed Kite and the Snail Kite, are now only seen in a small part of their former range. But for many species, the news is encouraging.

Hawks and eagles are now protected by law in the United States and Canada. Since DDT was banned in the 1970s, the numbers of Bald Eagles and Ospreys have been increasing. They are now seen across most of North America. Golden Eagles, Red-tailed Hawks, and Northern Harriers are also common in their ranges.

Nature has a way of finding its own balance. These magnificent birds of prey play a unique and important role. As long as we can preserve our woodlands, prairies, and wetlands, hawks and eagles and their relatives will soar high above us, patrolling the skies.

Friday—Teacher collects Team Page handouts, reviews key concepts, practices skills, and wraps up with the Closing.

Youth Church Meetings

Junior high youth groups will have special opportunities to develop events utilizing this manual. Youth ministry programs often have greater flexibility and broader goals than other agencies. Therefore, there is a great deal of flexibility in how these skill builders can be utilized. Two-hour youth nights at church would be able to accomplish the entire lesson, including a snack. The leadership of the lessons could easily be shared. Youth might also assist in the leadership for certain lessons. The lessons could also "stand alone," if certain core issues need addressing.

The authors recommend following the sequence of core lessons for personal development previously suggested (see "Core Lessons," p. 16).

Sunday School

This curriculum might be adaptable for a semester of youth Bible class or Sunday school. Since the Sunday format usually allows only one hour of time, the teacher would need to pick and choose carefully in order to capture the key learning from the lesson. Some lessons could be stretched out for two sessions on the same focus; an hour might be adequate for other lessons. A minicourse should include the recommended core lessons.

Weekend Retreats

The material is easily adaptable for a retreat or series of retreats. This suggested outline shows how one retreat might be designed:

Friday Night
1—Friendship (entire lesson)
Saturday
7—Self-Esteem (without Closing)
Break for outdoor recreation
Bonus Lesson 1—I Am What I Am: Discovering Personality Styles (without Presession or Warm-up)
Lunch
12—Listening, the Language of Friends: The Skill of Parroting (without Presession)
27—Put-Downs, Tear Downs (done outside; Bible Reflection done inside)

Supper
13—Listen for Feelings: The Key to Peer Relationships
27—Put-Downs, Tear Downs (Closing only)
Sunday Morning
Morning Worship
22—Talk to My Hand: Conflict Management (without Presession)
Break for outdoor recreation
24—Straight Up: Using "I Messages" (use abbreviated format)
Lunch
Departure

This schedule represents a busy timetable of learning that maximizes growth. To conduct a weekend with less class time, remove lessons 7, 27, 13, and 22. You would then need to design other structured outdoor activities and free time.

Five-Day Camp Programs

Camping ministry provides wonderful opportunities to focus on special skill-building and group development. The lessons can be woven into an active outdoor ministry, providing the theme and basis for learning sessions. Some Presessions and Closings could be eliminated.

Weekday Schedule

Monday
1—Friendship
7—Self-Esteem
Tuesday
Bonus Lesson 1—I Am What I Am: Discovering Personality Styles
12—Listening, the Language of Friends: The Skill of Parroting
Wednesday
18—Keep Talking: Conversation Openers
13—Listen for Feelings: The Key to Peer Relationships
Thursday
22—Talk to My Hand: Conflict Management
24—Straight Up: Using "I Messages"
Friday
Bonus Lesson 2—Measuring Your Listening Style
5—I've Got a Secret: Confidentiality

Friendship
Characteristics of a Friend

Introduction

A caring friend has the ability to make and keep friendships. Although young adolescents may make embarrassing mistakes and have tender feelings, they are also eager to explore friendships with greater independence and self-confidence. This lesson explores the value of commitment and sacrifice as important friendship qualities.

Key Concept

In John 15:13, Jesus says, "No one has greater love than this, to lay down one's life for one's friends. You are my friends if you do what I command you" (NRSV). Young adolescents are just beginning to discover what it takes to be a friend and stay friends.

Goals

Participants will explore some of the values and characteristics of friendship, rejoicing that Jesus has made them His friends through forgiveness and faith and that He strengthens their earthly friendships by His grace.

Bible Reference

The friendship story of Jonathan and David (1 Samuel 20)
Life-giving friendship in Jesus (John 15:12–15)

Lesson Overview

Activity	Summary	Goal	Materials	Time
Presession	Media friends	Provide a warm environment for youth as they arrive	Index cards	Arrival to starting time
Warm-up	Who's the Leader? game	An activity that builds group interaction	None	10 minutes
Focus	Know the secret for making friends	Jesus calls us friends	Index cards, pencils, masking tape	5 minutes
Activity	Top 10 list	Characteristics of friendship	Newsprint or chalkboard, marker or chalk, paper and pencils, colored adhesive dots	30 minutes
Bible Reflection	David and Jonathan	Story about faithfulness	Team Page, Bibles, pencils	20 minutes
Closing	Thank God for friends	Prayer stem completion	Candles	5 minutes

Presession: Media Friends

Write the names of famous friends on index cards. As youth arrive, shuffle the cards and then ask youth to match the pairs of friends. Time them to see who is fastest. Invite them to add new names. Here are a few famous friends:

Batman/Robin
Gilligan/Skipper
Popeye/Olive Oyl
Lucy/Ricky
Sylvester the Cat/Tweetie Bird
Blossom/Six
Tom/Jerry
Mickey Mouse/Minnie Mouse
Laurel/Hardy
Seinfeld/George Kastanza
Laura/Steve Erkel

Warm-Up

Play "Who's the Leader?" Ask the youth to sit in a circle on the floor. Join them and ask them to do everything you do. Perform simple motions that they are to follow. For example, you might pat your head, clap your hands, pull your ears, wave your hand, or cross your legs. Once the youth have practiced some motions, choose someone to be "it." While the "it" is out of sight, choose someone to be the leader. Instruct the leader to discreetly make motions for the group to follow. Invite the "it" to come back into the room and stand in the center of the circle. The leader tries to discreetly initiate motions for the group to follow. The goal is to keep the "it" from discovering who is the leader.

After playing several rounds, say, **This time let's make it very difficult for the "it." Let's all look at the leader as little as possible. Try to only glance at the leader or to look from the corner of your eye. When you see others change, you change too.**

Continue for a few more rounds.

Focus: The Secret to Making Friends

Divide the class into pairs. Give each pair pencils and an index card. Have each pair take three minutes to identify their version of the number one secret to making friends. Call time, and have students read their secret and then tape their card to the wall.

Activity: The Top 10

Tell the youth that they are going to help you find the top 10 friendship characteristics.

- Ask the youth to write down two or three qualities they look for in a friend.
- Ask them to each share a characteristic from their list as you record them all on newsprint or a chalkboard.
- Give each youth five colored, adhesive signal dots or a marking pen. Ask them to place a dot or mark next to their personal "top five" on the master list you have made.
- Tabulate the marks and make a list of the top 10 friendship characteristics.

Ask the group these questions:
- Based on our list, how would you evaluate this class as a friend-based group?
- What gets in the way?
- What are you going to do about it?

Bible Reflection: Team Page

Say, **Please form groups of four or five people. Be sure to include everyone. You will need your Bibles, the Team Page, and pencils. Choose someone to be the leader.** Tell the youth to transfer the class "top 10" to their Team Page. **Read each of the Bible passages in the column and then draw a star on the corresponding line for each of the qualities you find in that passage. You will have only 15 minutes to discuss the four passages and fill in the chart.**

Have groups report back. Encourage them to give a brief account of what is happening in each section of the story. Ask them, **What qualities from our list were demonstrated by Jonathan and David?** Have them draw a star on the Top 10 chart next to those qualities.

Closing

Close this section with a candle-lighting ceremony. Place as many candles on an altar as you have participants, with a large candle in the center. Light the large candle first and say, **Jesus is the light of the world. When you take your turn and light your candle, say, "The light of Christ's friendship will shine through me when …"** and complete the sentence by saying something specific you will do to show friendship in the coming week. For example, **"The light of Christ's friendship will shine through me when I talk to the new girl who has a locker by mine."**

Top 10 Friendship Characteristics

Friendship Characteristics *(Fill in the Top 10 list your class voted on.)*	1 Samuel 17:57–18:4	1 Samuel 19:1–4	1 Samuel 20:9–17	1 Samuel 31:1–4; 2 Samuel 1:10–12
1				
2				
3				
4				
5				
6				
7				
8				
9				
10				

Draw a star ☆ on the Top 10 chart next to those qualities that you find in today's Bible story.

Christians are the best at being friends.

What does Jesus mean in John 15:12–17? How did He demonstrate this kind of friendship for us? What can we do in this friendship?

Complete the following:
The light of Christ's friendship will shine through me when I

_____

_____

2 Inclusion

Showing Acceptance of Others

Introduction

Caring friends create an atmosphere of warm acceptance. Christian groups can easily become exclusive. Jesus sets the example of caring for those who are "outside" the group.

Key Concept

God cares about the lost. We are to model God's care in our relationships with others.

Goals

The youth will experience several simulations of exclusion to better understand what it feels like to be excluded, and then learn ways to be more inclusive.

Bible Reference

Jesus leaves the 99 and seeks the one that is lost (Luke 15:4–7).

Presession

Invite the youth to choose the music played before class. Have a good sound system and CD player prepared. Allow students to bring a wide selection of CDs—contemporary Christian, heavy metal, country, grunge, alternative, rap, classical, and others—or invite a small group to suggest selections in advance. Be careful to choose selections that are not offensive.

Lesson Overview

Activity	Summary	Goal	Materials	Time
Presession	Music group	Help youth see diversity of tastes	CD player and popular CDs	First arrival to starting time
Warm-up	Circle of Friends game	Create simulations of exclusion	Optional: video camera and whistle	15 minutes
Focus	What were the feelings of exclusion?	Process feelings and introduce the theme	Chalkboard or newsprint, chalk or marker, paper and pencils, optional video playback	15 minutes
Activity	The In Group game	Another simulation of inclusion, exclusion	Choose several students before class	15 minutes
Bible Reflection	Lost baseball player and lost sheep	Read two stories, then tell their own	Team Page, paper and pencils	20 minutes
Closing	The Holy Huddle	Encourage reaching out	Bible, Team Page	5 minutes

Presession (cont.)

As the youth arrive, ask them to make a selection from the list you have prepared. Write down their choices and include them on the playlist.

Warm-Up: Circle of Friends Game

Invite everyone to gather in an open recreation area. Say to the students, **During this game, I would like you to pay attention to your feelings. Awareness of your feelings is important. When I call out a number, you must link arms to form groups that have that exact number of people. Any people left out of a circle must sit out. We will play until there are only two people standing.**

Suggestion: You may need a whistle for this noisy activity. Be aware that youth may experience hurt feelings from this game.

Focus

If possible, use a video camera to record and view the game. Take some close-up shots of the people who are left out. Distribute paper and pencils. While students are watching the video, have them write down words for the different feelings they observe. If you choose not to videotape the exercise, ask them to recall all the different feelings they observed while playing the game. After they have written the feelings down, collect and record the list on the chalkboard or newsprint.

Activity

Play a game called the In Group. Before the activity, select several students to whom you will give a secret code. The secret is that they use their initials to choose items for a picnic. For example, Kurt Bickel, one of the authors, would bring a kite (for Kurt) and a ball (for Bickel). (The secret is that each person selects items that begin with the same letter as their initials.) Chairs should be in a circle. Say, **I'm going on a picnic and all those who belong to the "in group" can join me. You must bring the right things to this picnic. I'm bringing** (name two items that begin with your initials). **Who can join me?**

The leader sits in the center of the circle while others stand outside. When someone says the sentence correctly, the leader says, **You can now join the group!** They are then seated in

the circle. Again the leader repeats, **Who else can join?**

Allow frustration to build for those who do not know what is going on. You might say things such as

- The solution is so easy—once you know it, you'll be so embarrassed.
- I have played this with kindergarten children who have figured it out.
- You probably aren't listening very closely.

Give them a clue or two.

- Tell them to listen very carefully to what is being said.
- Say in a smug tone, **Here is a great clue: some people won't get this game *initially*.**

End the game and tell everyone what the secret is.

Say to the participants, **This game makes a point. Before you guess the point, think about your feelings at the beginning, in the middle, and at the end of the game.**

Bible Reflection

Form teams of four to six participants. Distribute the Team Page handout, and allow eight minutes to complete Teamwork Part A on a separate sheet of paper.

Ask them to complete Teamwork Part B. Allow 10 minutes.

Closing

Say to the students, **Some have described the church as "the Holy Huddle." Let's demonstrate what they mean. Would you** (point to about half the class) **please get up and demonstrate what a football huddle looks like?** (Wait until they make the huddle.) Ask the other half of the class to stay seated. Then ask, **As you look at this model, tell why the team huddles this way. How does the church huddle in the same way? What feelings does our church give new people? What are some clues that tell you whether people are feeling welcome or not? What are some ways we could change this?**

Continue, **Stay in your huddle as I read the Bible passage: Luke 15:4–7.** Have the huddle turn and face out. Ask those in the huddle to find someone not in the huddle and form a new circle with everyone looking out. Join hands and pray the prayer from the Team Page.

Teamwork
Part A

Thinking about the In Group game, write your answers to the following questions:
- How did you feel about the leader?
- How did you feel about kids who knew the secret when you didn't?
- How did you feel when you figured out the secret?
- How did you feel about the game?

Imagine you were outside the family of faith; how would that be like the game?
How is it different?

Teamwork
Part B

Read these next two stories aloud in your group.

Prepare to tell a story of your own by writing notes in the place provided. Tell a real story about being lost or on the outside of a friendship group.

Story #1

The baseball team had 19 players. No one thought much about it except Juan. Juan was the third-string right fielder. There were two players in every other spot. "Why did right field have to have three players?" Juan thought. "The coach will hardly miss me if I skip practice. It doesn't matter much. I never play in the games anyway."

Several hours later the doorbell rang. Juan could not believe his eyes when he opened the door and saw the coach standing there. "Where were you?" Coach asked.

"I didn't feel like going," Juan mumbled. "I didn't think you would miss me."

"Of course I missed you, Juan. Just because you are not a starting player does not mean you're not important to the team. I thought you might be feeling down so I wanted to stop by. Will you be there next week?"

Story #2

Which one of you, having a hundred sheep and losing one of them, does not leave the ninety-nine in the wilderness and go after the one that is lost until he finds it? When he has found it, he lays it on his shoulders and rejoices. And when he comes home, he calls together his friends and neighbors, saying to them, "Rejoice with me, for I have found my sheep that was lost." Just so, I tell you, there will be more joy in heaven over one sinner who repents than over ninety-nine righteous persons who need no repentance. (Luke 15:4–7 NRSV)

Sin ruins relationships. How does Jesus Christ seek, welcome, befriend, and involve us? What does it mean that He seeks us when we are lost? Into what groups does He welcome us?

Notes to Prepare a Similar Story

Prayer

May the God of steadfastness and encouragement grant you to live in harmony with one another, in accordance with Christ Jesus, so that together you may with one voice glorify the God and Father of our Lord Jesus Christ. Welcome one another, therefore, just as Christ has welcomed you, for the glory of God. Amen. (Romans 15:5–7 NRSV)

Hanging With

Peer Relationships

Introduction

Youth have different people throughout their lives who influence them. This session takes a look at the importance of these influences and evaluates positive and negative effects.

Key Concept

Identify what makes someone a positive support person.

Goals

Youth will see that a network of people influences their lives. They will identify characteristics of positive and negative influences.

Bible Reference

The Book of Ruth

Presession: Under the Influence

Post newsprint on the wall. As youth arrive, have them create a mural of everything that influences them. This can be done in words with crayon or marking pens, or with magazine pictures. The mural should include things like music, television or other media, wealth, and so on. Entitle the mural "Under the Influence."

Lesson Overview

Activity	Summary	Goal	Materials	Time
Presession	Youth will list all influences on mural	Heighten awareness of who/what influences them	Newsprint, markers and crayons, magazines	Arrival to start of session
Warm-up	Game of Bombardment	Associate watching for ball with influences	Nerf ball	15 minutes
Focus	Students name influences	Identify positive and negative influences	None	10 minutes
Activity	Youth identify influences and support	You are a composite of the relationships you have	Team Page, pencils	10 minutes
Bible Reflection	Ruth made choices that affected her whole life	See positive influences in the Bible story	Team Page	10 minutes
Closing	Youth share positive qualities about each other	Youth are built up by each other	Chair	15 minutes

Warm-Up: Bombardment

Divide into two groups. One team forms a circle around the other team, with enough room for them to move freely. Play the game of Bombardment like this: the outside circle of youth tries to tag the team inside the circle by throwing a Nerf ball at them. If the Nerf ball hits an individual, that person must join the outer circle. When the team inside the circle is down to only one person, the teams switch roles and play again. The last person in the circle from each group is the winner.

Focus: Duck, Duck

Youth will take a look at positive and negative influences in their life. Say, **Just like in the game of Bombardment, we are hit on all sides by things that affect us. All throughout your life you have been influenced by people and things. Share some examples of things that influenced you when you were young.** Allow time to respond. Parents, teachers, and other adults should be mentioned. Then say, **How have the influences changed since you were a child?** Allow time to reflect and respond. Then say, **What are some of the good things about the people who influence us? What are some of the things we need to watch out for? What does this statement mean to you: "You are a composite of the relationships you have"?** An old saying states, **"If it looks like a duck, walks like a duck, and quacks like a duck, it must be a duck." What does this saying mean? What are the negative aspects of this statement? How might the statement be true?**

What makes someone a negative influencer? Lead the conversation to conclude that much negativity is based on thoughtlessness, selfishness, and insensitivity toward others. Help students examine why a negative influencer may seem fun to be around.

What does a positive influencer look like? Look for responses about care for oneself and others.

Discuss these questions:

- Why is it important to recognize negative and positive influences?
- How do you fight negative influences?
- Why would it be important to have a positive group of people in your life no matter how old you are?
- How can you be a positive influence on someone else?

Remind students that the people they choose to hang around with can influence their choice of behaviors. The more they like themselves, the less likely that they will be influenced by negative sources.

Activity: People Bombardment

Use the Team Page, Teamwork Part A, and have students make a "mind map" of all the people who influence their lives. Draw your own map as an example for them. Explain, **The circle in the center should be you. You may add or take away the circles as you see fit. Place the names of people who influence you in the circles around you, along with a word that describes that person or their behavior.**

After youth have completed their maps of the present, ask them to make a map of the people who they might need to have around them in the future. Examples: boss, mentors, wife/husband, and so forth. Emphasize the importance of choosing positive people in their circle of influencers no matter what stage of life they are in. If there is a negative influencer in their circle now, they need to think about how they are handling that influence. Are they like the duck?

Bible Reflection

Read the summary of the Book of Ruth on the Team Page, Teamwork Part B, and discuss who influenced Ruth and whom she influenced. Discuss these questions: What characteristics of friendship did God work in her life? How has our forgiveness through faith in Jesus Christ brought influence to your life? How is our life in Christ further influenced by the power of God's Word and the work of the Holy Spirit? What traits of a good friend does the Gospel create in our lives?

Closing: Word Bombardment

Seat one student in a chair so his/her back is to the rest of the group. Have the group say words (positive) that come to their minds when they think of that person. Allow only one minute per person. Make sure each person has a turn in the chair.

"You are a composite of the relationships you have."

Teamwork Part A

Mind Map of those who influence your life today:

Who will influence you as you grow older?

Teamwork Part B: Bible Reflection

{1} In the days when the judges ruled, there was a famine in the land, and a certain man of Bethlehem in Judah went to live in the country of Moab, he and his wife and two sons. {3} But Elimelech, the husband of Naomi, died, and she was left with her two sons [Mahlon and Chilion]. {4} These took Moabite wives; the name of the one was Orpah and the name of the other Ruth. When they had lived there about ten years, {5} both Mahlon and Chilion also died, so that the woman was left without her two sons and her husband. {6a} Then she started to return with her daughters-in-law from the country of Moab. {7} So she set out from the place where she had been living, she and her two daughters-in-law, and they went on their way to go back to the land of Judah. {8} But Naomi said to her two daughters-in-law, "Go back each of you to your mother's house. May the Lord deal kindly with you, as you have dealt with the dead and with me." {16} But Ruth said, "Do not press me to leave you or to turn back from following you! Where you go, I will go; where you lodge, I will lodge; your people shall be my people, and your God my God. {17} Where you die, I will die—there will I be buried. May the Lord do thus and so to me, and more as well, if even death parts me from you!" {18} When Naomi saw that she was determined to go with her, she said no more to her. {19a} So the two of them went on until they came to Bethlehem.

(Ruth 1 NRSV)

4 Who's in Charge?
Influence and Control

Introduction

Proactive people focus their efforts on things they can influence before something negative happens. Reactive people focus their efforts on circumstances over which they have no control. Their focus results in blaming and increased feelings of victimization. Caring friends understand the difference between influence and control.

"The negative energy generated by [a person's] focus [on uncontrollable circumstances], combined with neglect in areas they could do something about, causes their Circle of Influence to shrink." (Stephen R. Covey, *The Seven Habits of Highly Effective People*)

Key Concept

Understanding the difference between influence and control allows us to avoid being negatively controlled, and opens opportunities for us to have a positive caring influence on our friends.

Goals

Participants will explore the difference between influence and control. They will explore their relationships considering who uses control and who uses influence. They will celebrate their relationship with a heavenly Father who chooses to influence even though He could control.

Lesson Overview

Activity	Summary	Goal	Materials	Time
Presession	You're getting warmer	Warm up the group and introduce the theme	"Good" item, "evil" item	First arrival to start of session
Warm-up	Guidelines	Nonverbal team exercise	Blindfold, ball, belt with ropes (see instructions)	20 minutes
Focus	Who is really in charge?	Teach the difference between controllers and influencers	Team Page	5 minutes
Activity	Group discussion	Identify controllers and influencers	Team Page, pencils	10 minutes
Bible Reflection	The Good Shepherd	God chooses to be an influencer	Team Page	10 minutes
Closing	Confession	Confess our misuse of power	Teachers Guide	10 minutes

Bible Reference

The Good Shepherd (John 10:11–15 NRSV)

Presession: You're Getting Warmer

As youth arrive, ask them to be seated in a circle. When a few have gathered, have one person leave the room so that they cannot hear what is being said inside your meeting place. Show the group two items that you are going to hide in the room. One item (a beer can, cigarette, or sharp knife) represents evil influences. The second item should be a Bible, representing good influences. Have everyone who has a birthday between January and June be on the "evil" side. Have everyone who has a birthday in July through December be on the "good" side. Hide the two items while everyone in the room watches. The two groups are to direct the student outside to their item by saying, "You're getting warmer" or "You're getting colder." No other directions are allowed.

Bring the person back in the room and tell them that the two groups are going to give directions toward one of two items. The person's task is to decide which influence to follow. Say "Go" and let the shouting of directions begin. Let the activity go on until one of the two items is found or five minutes are up.

Interview the person who was being influenced about how it felt to hear different voices shouting opposite directions.

Warm-Up: Guidelines

Collect the following items before class to accomplish the Warm-up activity. You will need
- A Nerf football or a soccer ball
- A blindfold
- A belt that would fit anyone in the class
- Four to six eight-foot pieces of rope. Tie the end of each rope onto the belt.

Divide the class into groups. Blindfold one person in one group, and have that person wear the belt. Each group member takes the end of one of the ropes so that the group is spread out in a circle around the one wearing the belt. Place the Nerf ball someplace in the room. Without speaking, have the group SAFELY work together, moving the person by manipulating the ropes, until she or he can pick up the ball. Then have the next team try. Time how long it takes for each team to get the ball. Make sure everyone participates in the experience.

Focus: Who Is Really in Charge?

Say, Perhaps there are times you feel like the person in the middle. Many people in your life attempt to control or influence you. And there are times you also try to control or influence others too. The truth is that you only have control over yourself and can only attempt to influence others. Distribute the Team Page. Describe influencers and controllers.

Activity

Have students independently complete the Teamwork section of the Team Page. Allow them to share their answers in small groups. Ask the whole class, How do you feel about control and your life? How do you feel about influence? Where does God fit in this picture?

Bible Reflection: Team Page

Ask youth to read the passage and consider whether Jesus is a controller or an influencer. Discuss the questions with the entire class.

Closing

Close with a confession of how we have misused power to control others.

Jesus is the only one who can truly control the entire universe. Yet He chose to influence us with His love and word of truth. People who have very little control often use a false sense of power to manipulate and subjugate others. Forgive us, Jesus, when we forget we are the sheep of the Good Shepherd. Amen.

Controller = orders, threatens, praises, punishes, and gives you no choice

A controller says, "I'm warning you. If you don't ... , I'll ... . I'll give you ... , if you'll ... ."

Influencer = suggests, teaches, advises, shares, and gives you a choice

An influencer says, "Have you considered ... ? Would this help? Here is what I learned about ... . I'd like to show you ... . I'd like to ask you to consider ... ."

Teamwork

Complete the following and share your answers with your group.

Who controls me? _____

_____

Who influences me? _____

_____

Whom do I control? _____

_____

Whom do I influence? _____

_____

Bible Reflection

I am the good shepherd. The good shepherd lays down his life for the sheep. The hired hand, who is not the shepherd and does not own the sheep, sees the wolf coming and leaves the sheep and runs away—and the wolf snatches them and scatters them. The hired hand runs away because a hired hand does not care for the sheep. I am the good shepherd. I know my own and my own know me, just as the Father knows me and I know the Father. And I lay down my life for the sheep. (John 10:11–15 NRSV)

How does a thief rob us of freedom? What kinds of influences "steal" people? All authority was given to Jesus. According to the above passage, how is His authority used to control and/or influence others? When and how does Jesus seek us out? How does it make you feel to know that He loves and cares for you?

4

Scripture: © NRSV. © 1999 CPH

I've Got a Secret
Confidentiality

Introduction

Friends share many kinds of information. A caring friend listens carefully to what is shared. Some information is public. Other information is private. A caring friend needs to know the difference and show loving care by keeping private things confidential. A caring friend also needs to consider whether private information *should* be told to someone in authority because of the risk of personal danger.

Key Concept

Caring friends should keep information confidential unless there are life-threatening circumstances. It is important to know when and when not to keep secrets and how to respond in any situation.

Goals

Youth will gain an appreciation for information that should be confidential and information that needs to be shared. They will practice recognizing the difference.

Bible Reference

Matthew 18:14–18

Lesson Overview

Activity	Summary	Goal	Materials	Time
Presession	A little-known fact about you	Youth share something about self	Slips of paper and pencils, box	First arrival to start of session
Warm-up	Guess who?	Youth learn names and something new about each other	Team Page, pencils	20 minutes
Focus	Introduce the lesson	Confidentiality is important for good, caring friends, but there are limits too	None	5 minutes
Activity	To tell or not to tell?	Youth discuss which things should stay secret and which should be told to an adult	Team Page, pencils	15 minutes
Bible Reflection	Matthew 18, the process for Christian confrontation	Youth learn what Jesus said to do when you have a concern about others' behavior	Team Page, pencils	15 minutes
Closing	Prayer	To identify "hot" issues and know that God cares about them	None	8 minutes

Presession: A Little-Known Fact

As youth arrive, ask them to write a little-known fact about themselves on the paper you provide. After they have written the fact, they should fold it and put it in the box you have prepared.

Warm-Up: Guess Who?

After everyone has completed the Presession activity, distribute the Team Page. Tell students to write the names of everyone in the class on the back of the Team Page. Go around the group asking each person to say their name so no one is left out.

Get the box of papers with the little-known facts. Read each one, allowing the youth to guess who may have written it. They should write a key word behind each name. For example, if the paper says, "I took piano lessons for three years," you should write "piano" behind the name of the person you think wrote it.

After you have read all the facts, go around one last time, asking the person who wrote it to stand up. The youth should circle their correct guesses.

Focus: Secrets

Announce, **Today we are going to talk more about helping others. When you listen to someone, you are helping them to solve their problems. When people tell you things about their feelings, it is important to keep that a secret between the two of you. That helps them to trust you and also lets them know you listen because you care, not because you want the latest gossip.**

Some secrets are not good to keep. When someone tells you about things that are life-threatening, you should tell them that it is unfair for you to keep the secret. Ask their permission to tell another responsible adult about it. If permission is not given, you may need to inform them that you must tell someone. Life-threatening situations include those involving unsafe sex, use of drugs, any reference to suicide or abuse, or criminal activity of any kind.

Activity: To Tell or Not to Tell?

Ask the youth to work in groups of four to six. They should discuss each situation from Teamwork Part B on the Team Page and then make a group decision.

Bible Reflection: Team Page

The Bible gives us a process for confronting someone who is behaving in a way that could hurt themselves or others. Read the passage on the Team Page and outline in your own words what it says. Discuss the questions with the entire class.

Closing

Close with a "popcorn prayer." The leader will say three phrases, and participants fill in one or more brief responses. The leader phrases are

- Lord, thank You for these gifts from You …
- Lord, give us wisdom when people talk to us about problems like …
- Lord, thank You for these trusted youth and adults …
- In Jesus' name. Amen.

Teamwork Part A: Guess Who?

Write the names of everyone in your class on the back of this page.

Teamwork Part B: To Tell or Not to Tell?

Work as a team and decide which of the following you would tell a responsible adult about and which you would not tell to anyone. Circle what you decide.

What people tell you ...

1	"I saw someone selling drugs on campus."	Tell	Don't Tell
2	"My girlfriend broke up with me and I'm feeling rotten."	Tell	Don't Tell
3	"I cheated on a test."	Tell	Don't Tell
4	"I have been caught shoplifting."	Tell	Don't Tell
5	"I wish my parents would get off my back."	Tell	Don't Tell
6	"I don't want to eat any lunch. I never do."	Tell	Don't Tell
7	"I can't stand that teacher."	Tell	Don't Tell
8	"I wish I were someone else."	Tell	Don't Tell
9	"I know who likes Tasha."	Tell	Don't Tell
10	"Sometimes I think about killing myself."	Tell	Don't Tell

Remember ... if in doubt about confidentiality, ask the friend if you can share the information. If necessary, ask a trusted adult for advice without mentioning names.

Bible Reflection

Read the passage below and outline the process for confronting a friend.

It is not the will of your Father in heaven that one of these little ones should be lost. If another member of the church sins against you, go and point out the fault when the two of you are alone. If the member listens to you, you have regained that one. But if you are not listened to, take one or two others along with you, so that every word may be confirmed by the evidence of two or three witnesses. If the member refuses to listen to them, tell it to the church; and if the offender refuses to listen even to the church, let such a one be to you as a Gentile and a tax collector. Truly I tell you, whatever you bind on earth will be bound in heaven, and whatever you loose on earth will be loosed in heaven. (Matthew 18:14–18 NRSV)

What kind of "faults" might be dealt with in this manner? Why would you keep a "fault" to yourself? How often might you try to deal with the issue privately? When do you move on to the next step? Why? What is the final outcome of this process? How does God's love and forgiveness motivate what is told to others and not told?

6 In a Crisis
Taking Steps to Help

Introduction

CPR saves lives when people are in physical need. Things can be just as dramatic when people are in an emotional crisis. This session will introduce youth to four steps of action when a peer experiences emotional crisis. Crises can include thoughts of suicide, drug use, and physical and/or emotional abuse. All are serious situations. All are part of youth culture. Youth can minister to others by knowing what to do in times of crisis, and they can literally save lives.

Key Concept

Youth often turn to their friends first when encountering situations they find overwhelming or depressing. Youth will identify four concrete steps in the helping process.

Goals

Youth will gain confidence in knowing what to do in critical emotional situations.

Bible Reference

Hebrews 13:8

Presession: Tough Times

Using newspapers and magazines, have youth find photos and articles that portray serious emotional challenges. Cut them out and make a collage on a piece of poster board.

Lesson Overview

Activity	Summary	Goal	Materials	Time
Presession	Clipping news stories of crises	Introduce the topic	Newspapers, old magazines, scissors, tape, poster board	First arrival to start of session
Warm-up	"Standing Outside the Fire"	Listen to the music and discuss the meaning	CD or tape of the selected music and a play-back unit	10 minutes
Focus	Lecture on what to do when things go wrong	Teaching basic principles for managing a crisis	Student responses on newsprint, marker	10 minutes
Activity	Reinforce crisis management with four steps	Youth take notes about the four steps to take in a crisis	Team Page, pencils, student responses from Focus	15 minutes
Bible Reflection	Hebrews 13:8	Youth express their thoughts in a poem	Team Page and pencils, newsprint and markers	15 minutes
Closing	Poems		Poems from Bible Reflection	10 minutes

Warm-Up: "Standing Outside the Fire"

Have the Garth Brooks song "Standing Outside the Fire" cued up as youth arrive. Read the words aloud before you play the song and encourage the youth to sing along. Discuss possible meanings of this song or any other similar songs the youth can recall.

Focus: What to Do When Things Go Wrong

The first person that youth turn to in a crisis is often a friend. The friend may be uncertain of how to respond, especially when the situation is serious or life-threatening. Ask youth to share situations they have already encountered or have "heard about." Say, **We live in a complex world. People your age have many issues confronting them. Think of situations you have to deal with that your parents may not have encountered.** List some of these situations on newsprint. **Who might you turn to when you need help sorting out things that are bothering you?** Most will say their friends; some will say parents or teachers. **Most people your age turn first to their friends when they are facing situations that are very difficult and depressing. If you are the friend, this may make you uncomfortable. You may not know what to do. Today we will talk about some specific things you can do to help your friends. Although normal, everyday issues are important, in this session we are going to discuss what you can do when you or your friends encounter issues such as suicide, drug abuse, physical or emotional abuse, or eating disorders.**

Share some current examples of youth in danger. Then ask, **What are some things you can do when someone comes to you with a serious, life-threatening situation?** List the suggestions on newsprint. Don't forget to include reading the Bible and praying together. Christ is our solid rock in a changing and frightening world. **All of these suggestions are on target. Now let's look at the four steps to take when your friends are in trouble and come to you for help.**

Activity: Make a Plan

Hand out the Team Page. Compare their suggestions from the Focus section to the four steps listed on the page. Go over each step indi-vidually and discuss. Tell students that they may take notes.

Say, **These steps are basic suggestions to get you started. Many alternatives can be included within each step. The first step is to take each situation seriously. Some situations may sound silly at first, but your friends may simply be "bouncing" the idea off you to get your reaction. When someone is desperate enough to consider suicide, they may not be thinking rationally and may say or do things that serve as hints. Suicide victims may leave a note, but they don't always do so. Whether your friend is considering suicide or is involved in drugs, a change in their normal behavior is common. Friends involved in drugs may hang out with other users and drop their previous friendships. Friends who are considering suicide may suddenly withdraw or be deeply depressed much of the time. Victims of abuse may withdraw or "act out," publicly expressing rebellion. Any change of behavior that seems out of place should be noted. If you are worried that a friend may be considering suicide, ask if they are thinking of hurting themselves. Sometimes this question is a relief, as it invites them to talk about their problem.**

The second step is to assure them of alternative choices and refer them to help that is readily available. Be a good, active listener, but do not allow yourself to be their sole source of strength. Assure them that you will "be there" for them, but remind them that there are others who care and want to help. Point out that Christ Himself went through tough times, and reassure them He is also with them now. It is important to stay in contact until you can get them help. Don't be afraid to share your faith and pray with them if they are open to it.

Step three involves finding a responsible adult whom they feel comfortable talking to. This may be difficult if they see you as the only help they need. While your help is important, you must not see yourself as their rescuer. You must help them find an adult who can help share responsibility for their life. The best thing is to have them contact someone for help. They may consent to your setting up an appointment with an adult. Try to avoid making a promise that you will not tell about the situation; if you have already made that promise, explain to them

that you care too much about their well-being not to find help for them. After all, if they have told you, they really do want someone to help. You must ask yourself, "What if I kept the secret and they hurt themselves or others? How would I feel then?" They may still choose to continue their behavior, remain in their environment, or act inappropriately, but at least you tried to help them.

The last step is to follow up. After you have helped them connect with an adult, check back to let them know that you still care. Staying in touch shows them that they can still count on you as a friend who will not dump them just because they shared a problem.

This is a heavy topic. Have the youth form teams of two. Have partners lean against one another, back to back, and see if they can sit down without using their hands. Then see if they can get up the same way. Now have them lock elbows and repeat the process. Then have them bend over to lift the other slightly off the floor. Next, have them face each other and join palms above their heads, seeing how far they can step back with their feet, using their hands as a brace. Remind students that using each other as support in friendships means that you are there for each other through some hard times.

Bible Reflection: Jesus Never Changes

Read Hebrews 13:8 from the Team Page, Teamwork Part B. Break youth into groups of three. Ask for situations in which someone might wonder if Jesus is there. Discuss how it feels to know that Jesus will never change His attitude of love and forgiveness for them. Have students write a poem reflecting their feelings about supporting friends who may be going through difficult times. Haiku poetry might be a good format.

A Haiku poem has just three unrhymed lines. The first and third lines have five syllables. The middle line has seven syllables. All three lines center around a theme. Some poets enjoy contrasting three different approaches to the same theme.

Have them rewrite their poems on newsprint and display.

Closing: Poems to Praise

Share the Haiku poems, and summarize the thoughts in a prayer.

Teamwork Part A

Four Helping Steps

1. Take your friend's problem seriously.

2. Assure your friend that there is help available.

3. Get an adult involved.

4. Keep in touch with your friend.

Teamwork Part B: Bible Reflection

"Jesus Christ is the same yesterday and today and forever." (Hebrews 13:8 NRSV)

How does it feel to know that Jesus will never change His love for you? How does it feel to know that He will never change His location, but will stay with you always?

Example of a Haiku poem: three unrhymed lines, the first line with five syllables, the second with seven, and the third with five.

People, laughing, sad,
Doing the best that they can,
Sometimes need our help.

7 Self-Esteem

Introduction

The most important attribute of well-being is self-esteem. There are many factors that affect self-perspective. Self-esteem is a gift of God provided primarily through parents. Friends, siblings, and other significant adults also contribute to a youth's sense of well-being.

Key Concept

Christian self-esteem is rooted in the knowledge that God loves us with an unconditional love. God's love is demonstrated in Jesus Christ, and we share this news with others. God helps us accept His love, pass on His love, and receive His love when it is channeled through others.

Goals

Participants will see their role as God's ambassadors of love. The participants will practice giving and receiving affirmation, and explore ways to develop self-awareness.

Bible Reflection

The Ten Commandments begin with "You should not ... ." Jesus says the greatest commandments are about love—for God and for others (Mark 12:30–31).

"I have loved you with an everlasting love; therefore I have continued my faithfulness to you" (Jeremiah 31:3 NRSV).

Lesson Overview

Activity	Summary	Goal	Materials	Time
Presession	"This Is Me" poster	To create a welcoming atmosphere	Poster board, marking pens, instructions, your sample	Presession time
Warm-up	Group mingles about and shares posters, music playing in background	Develop community and a sense of inclusion	CD/tape player, selection of popular music, prepared posters	10 minutes
Focus	Tell a story	Provide a metaphor for positive sharing	Printed story with questions	10 minutes
Activity	Sharing meaning of posters	Giving and receiving positive affirmation	Posters the students created	15 minutes
Bible Reflection	Jesus gives a new command to love one another	Youth see their role in Jesus' vision of a loving people	Team Page, Bible, pencils	15 minutes
Note Passing	Play the game "Passing Notes"	Reinforce concept	Bible, Team Page, scrap paper for notes	15 minutes
Closing	Notes of appreciation to Jesus	A ritual of adoration for Jesus	Notes to Jesus, box, Team Page	5 minutes

Presession: "This Is Me" Poster

Make your own poster beforehand and display it as an example. Post these instructions for youth to create their own:

Create a poster about yourself (use only half of the page) using drawings and symbols to show

- Your name
- Something you do well
- Your best time of day
- Something you are proud of

Warm-Up

Gather everyone together and welcome them as VIPs—very important people.

Announce, **You are "very important people" to me. You are "very important people" to our church/school, and you are "very important people" to Jesus.**

Get your posters and form one large circle. Have every other youth step into the circle and turn to face out, creating two concentric circles facing each other. Play the music loud, while the outside circle walks clockwise and the inside circle walks counter-clockwise.

Periodically stop the music so that each person can show and discuss their poster with the person closest to them (one minute). Repeat the process until they have shared with at least four people.

Focus

Ask the youth to be seated. Announce that the theme for this lesson is self-esteem. Ask, **When you think about yourself, do you like yourself?** Allow responses, then say, **You should know that God likes you. Here is what He said in the Book of Jeremiah: "I have loved you with an everlasting love; therefore I have continued my faithfulness to you"** (Jeremiah 31:3 NRSV).

Listen to this story, so that we can discuss it in a few minutes as we talk more about self-esteem.

The Land of Buckets

Once there was a land where every person carried a bucket and a dipper. The bucket held crystal water, necessary for life. The dipper allowed them to give this water to others.

The Bucketeers, as they were known, felt comfortable with themselves and appreciated the uniqueness of others. They were positive and wonderful—as long as their buckets were full. When their buckets were low, their thoughts and feelings got worse. If their buckets ever ran out of the crystal water, they became miserable.

The dippers were made so that they could dip into their own bucket of water and pour a ladle-full into someone else's bucket. Incredibly, when that happened, their own water did not decrease. In fact, to their surprise, their supply would increase.

Many Bucketeers learned the secret of keeping a full bucket. Whenever they noticed someone with a low bucket, they would dip in and give some of their water away. When a child was born into the Land of Buckets, everyone would gather to make sure the new Bucketeer, born with an empty bucket, received lots of crystal water.

One day a Bucketeer noticed that his bucket had become empty. He decided that since he had no crystal water for giving, he would have to use his dipper for taking. When he snuck up and dipped into the bucket of one especially happy friend, the friend felt the loss of water and went away sad. The Bucketeer who had taken crystal water looked in his own bucket; strangely enough, although he had taken a full dipper, only a small amount of water had made it in. He became desperate, dipping into the buckets of others.

Unbeknownst to him, the full bucket of his friend was not replenished. Furthermore, when others saw the new use for the dippers, they began dipping too. The once-wonderful land was soon filled with people dipping into others' buckets for the crystal water.

Those few who remembered the secret kept their buckets full by using the dippers exclusively for giving, making themselves and others happy.

Discuss the meaning of the story.

- If the crystal water represents love, what does the dipper represent?
- How full are the buckets of people at school, at church, or in your family?
- Why do you think the Bucketeers could not keep the water they took from others?
- Why do you think the miserable Bucketeer had an empty bucket?
- What is especially sad about the end of the story?

Activity: Pass the Poster

Have students get their posters and form circles of four to six. Emphasize being kind and welcoming each other to the circle. Explain the following:

Make sure that your name is prominently displayed on your poster. Pass your poster to the person on your right. That person is to draw a word or symbol on the bottom half of the poster that describes a positive, unique characteristic about the creator of that poster. Pass the poster to each person around the circle.

Have the poster owner share with the whole group what he or she interprets the added words or symbols to mean.

Bible Reflection: Team Page

Tell the students the following:

Please form groups of four or five. Make sure to include everyone. For this exercise you need Bibles, the Team Page, and pencils. Choose a leader. You have only 15 minutes to discuss things in this segment.

Have students complete the two Teamwork sections. Talk about the way Jesus sums up the commandments in two statements. **Why might He have done this? What do the statements mean for us? I will be around if you have any questions.**

Monitor the teams and encourage everyone to participate. After sufficient time, or when their interest level decreases, move on to the next segment.

Note Passing in Class

Re-gather the class in a large group. Assign students to chairs in alphabetical order. In a fun manner, introduce the game "Passing Notes." Have students copy messages from the Team Page onto scrap paper, with an individual in mind for each message. Tell students that the goal is to pass as many affirming notes as possible without being caught by the teacher.

Announce to the class, **Class, I am going to read 1 Corinthians 13 out loud. While I do, make sure I don't catch you passing notes.**

Look down at first while you read, so they can pass notes.

Look up and discover a note. Have it brought forward and read it aloud. If it is a positive note, send the student to stand in a corner until someone else is "caught."

Repeat the process several times until they tire of playing.

Then announce, **I would like you to prepare one last note to pass. This note is written to Jesus. Just think, if you had gone to school with Jesus, you might have sent Him a note. Write something positive you'd like to tell Him, and we will use the notes in our Closing.**

Closing

Stand in a circle shoulder to shoulder. (Remember to bring the notes to Jesus.) Place a box in the center of the circle. Read your note first, then place it into the box. Have everyone else follow your example. Allow students to place their note in the box without reading it aloud. Close with the prayer printed on the Team Page.

Other Resources

An alternative to the Buckets story is on page 51 of *Tell Me the Secrets* by Max Lucado, illustrated by Ron DiCianni. Published by Crossway Books, Wheaton, Illinois, ISBN 0-80107-730-8. It is available in many Christian bookstores.

Teamwork Part A

Work in teams to complete the following:

We often use mirrors to try to gain a clearer self-concept.

Who on your team spends the most time in front of a mirror?

_____

For what are mirrors useful? Think of some creative new uses for mirrors. What can't a mirror show us about ourselves?

_____

_____

Read the following Bible passages. What do you see? What do they tell you about yourself? What do they tell you about God?

Romans 5:8 _____

_____

Jeremiah 31:3 _____

_____

John 15:15 _____

_____

Teamwork Part B: Read It!

Jesus said, "You shall love the Lord your God with all your heart, and with all your soul, and with all your mind, and with all your strength. ... You shall love your neighbor as yourself. There is no other commandment greater than these" (Mark 12:30–31 NRSV).

List three positive actions you might do in each category below.

Love One Another
Love for God
with all your heart, soul, mind, and strength

Love for Each Other
Love your neighbor as you love yourself

A Prayer for Self-Esteem

Dear Father, You are the best. You have loved us with an unending love. Even though You knew that we would be sinners, You sent Jesus to rescue us. Help us remember and celebrate Your love for us. Empower us by Your Spirit to love one another in Jesus' name. Amen.

Sentence Starters for Passing Notes

What I like about you is ...

You are important to our class because ...

It is fun to be with you because ...

8 Mood Swings
Four "Feeling Categories"

Introduction

Our moods may change for a number of reasons. Learning to success-fully handle mood swings is part of the maturing process. This lesson stresses that having different feelings is neither good nor bad; as we learn to control our moods and actions, we should also learn to accept the moods of others. An important part of caring friendships is learning how to help others cope with their feelings.

Key Concept

Recognizing that mood swings are a normal process of life helps us learn to control extreme feelings.

Goals

The participants will discuss their feelings and moods. They will learn that St. Peter also had different moods. They will consider ways to help others who are in depressed moods.

Bible Reference

Stories about Peter from the Gospels

Lesson Overview

Activity	Summary	Goal	Materials	Time
Presession	Create "Mood Room"	Welcome students and introduce theme	Various items to decorate the room in four different moods	First arrival to start of session
Warm-up	Mood continuum	Begin identifying the four basic moods	Word list from Teachers Guide	10 minutes
Focus	Guided recall	Youth remember their moods and get in touch with their feelings	Questions from the Teachers Guide	5 minutes
Activity	Your week of moods	Identify the ups and downs of their week	Team Page, pencils	15 minutes
Bible Reflection	St. Peter had highs and lows too	Chart St. Peter's possible moods on the chart	Team Page, Bibles, pencils	15 minutes
Closing	Mood music	Write down feelings inspired by the music and give thanks in prayer for feelings	Three or four recorded songs for playback; chalkboard or newsprint and writing implement	10 minutes

Presession: "Mood Room"

Make large signs to put on the wall or hang from the ceiling near each corner. Each sign should have one of the following labels: *Mad, Glad, Sad, Scared.* Put mural paper on the walls so the youth can draw and write according to the theme. Have balloons, magazines, music, and different lighting options available. As the youth arrive, ask them to help you decorate each corner of the room in the designated mood.

Warm-Up: Choose a Mood

Explain that you have created a four-corner mood continuum. The students should consider each of the corners and move to the place in the "mood room" that best describes how they feel when they hear each of the following words:

Math
Dating
Poverty
Joining a new group
The first day of school
Report card
A family trip
Discrimination
A pool party
Surgery
Pizza
Chores

Invite them to share briefly why they stand where they do.

Focus

Ask the youth to close their eyes and listen carefully to your voice as they reflect upon the following questions:
When is the last time you remember being sad or angry?
What happened to shape those feelings?
Can you see the people involved?
When did you stop feeling sad or angry?
What did you do to feel better?
How can we better manage our moods?
How can we help others manage their moods?

Activity

Ask the youth to form teams of three or four people. Give them the Team Page handout. Encourage them to complete Teamwork Part A and share it.

Bible Reflection

Explain how to complete Teamwork Part B on the Team Page handout. The students will need their Bibles.

Closing: Mood Music

Choose (or enlist students to help you choose) three or four different songs that describe feelings. Play samples of each song and have the youth describe the feelings the songs create in them. List all the feelings on a chalkboard or newsprint. Close with a prayer thanking God for being with us in all of our feelings (include those on the list).

Teamwork Part A

Make a chart of your moods during the last week.

Monday	Tuesday	Wednesday	Thursday	Friday	Saturday	Sunday

Identify one activity from the week, and determine whether it was positive or negative. What did you do to contribute to the negative or positive feelings?

Share with your group how your week went, especially some of your high and low points during the week.

Teamwork Part B

Read the following passages from your Bible and determine how Peter must have felt. Put your response in the space provided.

Mark 1:14–18	Matthew 14:22–32	Mark 9:2–9	Luke 22:54–62	John 21:15–19

8   Team Page *Mood Swings*

Feelings Fair
Feelings Are Important

9

Introduction

A caring friend is aware of feelings. It is healthy for all people to be able to express their own feelings and listen for feelings in others. Tom Rusk, M.D., says, "Feelings contain important information. [People] may feel awful, but [feelings] are never ridiculous or wrong, sinful or evil. And they should never be ignored." Feelings offer insight into the soul.

Key Concept

This lesson is designed to explore feelings and build a greater vocabulary for feeling words.

Goals

This lesson is designed to help youth understand that feelings are a precious gift from God, as the students explore additional, nonverbal ways to express feelings.

Bible Reference

"That very Spirit intercedes with sighs too deep for words" (Romans 8:26b NRSV).

Lesson Overview

Activity	Summary	Goal	Materials	Time
Presession	Hidden prize	Guessing game with a surprise	Three jars of small items (pennies, jelly beans, or M&Ms), candy bar or small toy, play dough	Before class time begins
Warm-up	Play-dough sculpture	Express feelings in artwork	Play dough for each person	10 minutes
Focus	Four main categories of feelings	The basic feelings have many forms of expression	Chalkboard or newsprint, jars from Presession	5 minutes
Activity	Feelings Fair	Youth express feelings	Six Feelings Centers (see details in manual), Team Page	30 minutes
Bible Reflection	Romans 8:22–28	Learn that God knows and understands our feelings	Team Page, pencils	10 minutes
Closing	Sentence stem completion and note to Jesus	Large group sharing	Team Page, box	10 minutes

Presession: Hidden Prize

Before the session, fill three glass jars with small items like pennies, jelly beans, or M&Ms. However, in the center of each jar hide a larger item like a big candy bar or a small toy wrapped in play dough. Count and record the number of items in each jar. Make a sign that says, "Guess the closest—win the jar!" As youth arrive, have them write down their estimate for each jar. Say, **We will announce the winners during this session.**

Warm-Up

Welcome everyone and announce that they will practice expressing their feelings in sculpture. Distribute play dough to each participant. Ask them to listen to the following stories and make something with the play dough that reflects their reaction to each one.

Read, **It is your first day at a new school. You moved to this city several weeks ago. You don't know anyone. You walk slowly from your parent's car toward the school entrance. You see lots of kids hanging in small groups. The bell rings and people scurry everywhere. You look for someone, anyone, who might show you where room B203 is.**

Give a few minutes for them to form the play dough into a shape that expresses their feelings. Have them describe their creation to three people. Then read the next story.

Your best friend just came to school looking totally out of it. You ask, "What's wrong?" and he bites his lip to hold back tears. "I don't want to talk about it." You know him too well to just let it go, so you say, "Come on! It can't be that bad." He snaps back at you, "Oh yeah, how would you like it if you found out your parents were getting a divorce as soon as the school year is over?"

Give students a few minutes to reshape the play dough to express their feelings. Have them describe their creation to three different people. Then read the following story.

It seems too good to be true. You have been talking, thinking, and praying about nothing else for a year now. And now, out of the blue, everything you wished for has come true. Things couldn't be better.

Give students two minutes to express their feelings in the play dough again. Have them share their creation with three different people.

Focus: Feelings Go Deep

Announce the winners of the guessing contest. Reveal the hidden objects. Ask, **How are these jars like feelings?** Give studens enough time to think, looking for answers such as "Hidden feelings are important," or "You can't always tell what people are feeling," or "Feelings are layered. If we only look at the surface we might miss the truth."

Write the words *mad, glad, sad,* and *scared* on the chalkboard or newsprint. Then say, **Basically there are only these four categories of feelings, yet there are many, many ways to express them. Our lesson will explore other ways of expressing feelings, including painting, sculpting, poetry, and short stories.**

Activity: Feelings Fair

Hand out the Team Page. Explain that the six booths or tables are places where students will learn to express their feelings in different ways. Have students move from place to place until they have completed at least four of the activities. Remind them that they should have the volunteer at each booth mark off each completed activity on their Team Page.

Booth #1 Birthday Feelings

Decorate the table with balloons and party favors. Have construction paper, scissors, and marking pens for making birthday cards. Have participants make a card for someone who will be having a birthday soon. Emphasize that they should express their feelings about that person in words and designs.

Booth #2 Friend Metaphor

Make a sign that says the following: "A metaphor describes things in picture language. An example is the psalmist David's description of his love for God: 'As a deer longs for flowing streams, so my soul longs for you, O God' (Psalm 42:1–2 NRSV). Create a metaphor comparing you and your best friend on the index card provided."

Decorate the table with a white paper tablecloth with words written in marking pens, such as *buddy, companion, comrade, pal, confidant, ally, compatriot, friend.*

Booth #3 Sad, Sad, Sad

Make a sign that says, "Draw the saddest day of your life, using colored chalk on black construction paper."

Decorate the table with a black table covering.

Booth #4 Pray, Praise, and Hooray!

This booth is for expressing feelings of thankfulness to God for the good things in our life.

Put up large pieces of mural paper on the wall. Provide drop cloths and other protection for the floor. Title the mural paper "Pray, Praise, and Hooray! (Express your feelings in color.)"

Provide brushes and watercolor paints for the youth to express their feelings of thankfulness. A CD or cassette player might play praise music at this booth.

Booth #5 Family Feelings

At this booth youth will make a pipe-cleaner sculpture of their family. Provide pipe cleaners and a cardboard square or a Styrofoam grocery tray as a stand. Have a sample or two available.

Booth #6 Photo Feelings

This booth might simulate the picture booths in the mall, using a Polaroid camera. Have youth pose for a picture in groups of four. Have each person show a different expression: mad, glad, sad, or scared. Post and have others guess the expressions.

Bible Reflection: Team Page

After everyone has experienced the Feelings Fair, bring students together with their handouts and say, **Turn to Teamwork Part B on your Team Page and look at the Bible passage from Romans. Answer the questions and move on to complete Teamwork Part C.**

Closing

Bring the group into a large circle and ask them to listen to each other as they complete the following sentence from the Team Page:

My name is _____ and during this class, I felt these three feelings:

_____

_____

_____.

In Teamwork Part C, students have written down their feelings for Jesus. Have students relate these feelings. Tear the sections off, fold them, and put them in a box. Have the whole group take them to the church altar. Pray about the feelings there, or have the pastor express the feelings in the Sunday petitions.

Other Resources

"White Rock Blues" video by Ray Cioni: This discussion starter is an animated fantasy giving important clues for discovering who you are and why you are here. After viewing, ask, **What does this video teach you about human nature? What does this video teach you about yourself? What does God's Word say about this topic?**

Teamwork Part A

Feelings Fair Checklist (get this page checked off at each booth)

Booth #1	Booth #2	Booth #3
Birthday Feelings Make a card for someone who will celebrate a birthday soon.	**Friend Metaphor** Write a metaphor about you and your best friend.	**Sad, Sad, Sad** Draw the saddest day of your life.
Booth #4	Booth #5	Booth #6
Pray, Praise, and Hooray! Express your feelings of thankfulness in color.	**Family Feelings** Create a pipe-cleaner sculpture of your family.	**Photo Feelings** Form groups of four. Have your picture taken with each person expressing a different emotion: mad, glad, sad, or scared.

Teamwork Part B

Read the following passage from Romans 8:22–28. Answer the questions at the end.

> We know that the whole creation has been groaning in labor pains until now; and not only the creation, but we ourselves, who have the first fruits of the Spirit, groan inwardly while we wait for adoption, the redemption of our bodies. For in hope we were saved. Now hope that is seen is not hope. For who hopes for what is seen? But if we hope for what we do not see, we wait for it with patience. Likewise the Spirit helps us in our weakness; for we do not know how to pray as we ought, but that very Spirit intercedes with sighs too deep for words. And God, who searches the heart, knows what is the mind of the Spirit, because the Spirit intercedes for the saints according to the will of God. We know that all things work together for good for those who love God, who are called according to his purpose. (NRSV)

If God knows your every thought and feeling, why does He allow us to have bad times and sad feelings? What gives the Christian hope? How does the life of Christ, including His suffering, death, and resurrection, give us strength?

Teamwork Part C

Write your response below and be prepared to share your feelings with the group:
My name is

_____

and during this class, I felt these three feelings:

_____

_____

_____

Dear Jesus, I have these feelings toward You …

What's Happening?
How to Say "No" to Risky Behavior

Introduction

Youth are bombarded with many choices that affect their personal lives, their families, and others around them. It is important to help them identify risky behaviors and be prepared to confront compromising situations, so that they might make better choices. This session focuses on tangible behaviors youth can choose when faced with difficult decisions.

Key Concept

Identify what constitutes risky behavior and teach students to creatively prepare specific alternate behavior choices.

Goals

Youth will recognize when they are in compromising situations and learn to remove themselves from the situation without "losing face."

Bible Reference

The Temptations of Jesus (Matthew 4:1–10)

Lesson Overview

Activity	Summary	Goal	Materials	Time
Presession	Collage of temptations	Raise awareness of various choices	Magazines, newspapers, scissors, glue or tape, newsprint	First arrival to start of session
Warm-up	Youth divide cards into risky and safe behaviors	Choose between risky and safe behavior	Set of cards from Teachers Guide, mural paper with line in middle, tape	10 minutes
Focus	Youth will explore options when in risky situations	Youth will learn to choose safer, alternate behaviors	Chalkboard or newsprint, writing implement	10 minutes
Activity	Youth will label risky behaviors	Identify behaviors as risky	Newsprint, drawing tools, set of cards, watch	15 minutes
Bible Reflection	Youth will apply Bible teachings to life	Youth will see Jesus as one who was also tempted	Team Page, pencils	10 minutes
Closing	Youth will practice getting out of difficult situations	Practice techniques	Team Page	15 minutes

Presession: Temptation Everywhere

Have students create a collage of magazine/newspaper headlines or photos depicting contemporary temptations that face youth. Tape or glue them onto newsprint for display purposes.

Warm-Up: This and That

Draw a line down the middle of a large piece of mural paper and fasten the paper to the wall. Write "Still Safe" on one side of the line and "Too Risky" on the other.

Prior to class time, reproduce the set of the cards that accompanies this lesson. (You will need one set for the Warm-up, and additional sets for the Activity.) Distribute cards to the youth, and have them tape their card to either side of the line, explaining why they made the decision that they did.

Focus: Risky Behaviors

Ask, **What makes behavior risky or safe?** Allow youth to respond. **On our newsprint you put behaviors that are considered healthy or safe on one side and behaviors considered to be risky on the other. How do you know when you are engaging in risky behavior?** Allow youth to discuss the criteria they used.

Focus the discussion on the students' feelings. This point should be made: if any trusted adult or authority might be upset with you for doing a certain behavior, it probably is in the "risky" category. **Why would you want to stay away from risky behavior?** Make the point that parents usually give more privileges to youth who choose positive behaviors. **Are there any advantages to engaging in risky behaviors?**

Today we are going to discuss risky behavior and explore ways you can say "no" to friends and still maintain their friendship, or "save face." How might you respond when your friends want you to do something that you know is wrong or dangerous? Make a list of things they suggest on a chalkboard or newsprint. Make sure the list includes the following:

- Be assertive. Say no. No explanation from you is necessary.
- Act shocked: "You know I would never choose to do that!"
- Walk away. Act distracted, like you didn't even hear them.

- Kiss up: "I know you are way too smart to try that."
- Make an excuse: "I've got to be home by ..."
- Make it into a joke: "Like I'm really going to do this and be grounded for the rest of my life."
- Remind them of someone they look down upon who did a similar thing.
- Say you are not feeling up to it.

Whatever tactic you use, it is very important to remove yourself physically from the situation. If it is impossible to remove yourself physically, then do so mentally or emotionally. (Read a book or magazine, look for something in your book bag, go to the bathroom, and so on.)

Activity: Pictionary Risks

Divide youth in teams of five or six. Two teams gather around a newsprint tablet. Have a set of cards available for every two teams. One youth picks a card and begins to illustrate the risky behavior on the newsprint. His team tries to guess what he is drawing. The other team uses a watch to call "time" after one minute. If the team doesn't guess properly, the other team has one guess. Alternate the process to the other team.

Title the newsprint pages and display them in art-gallery style around the classroom.

Bible Reflection: Been There, Done That

Distribute the Team Page for work on Teamwork Part A. Ask the youth to read the account of Jesus' temptations in Matthew 4:1–10.

Discuss what modern-day temptations parallel the temptations of Jesus. How did Christ handle it? Is there anything we can learn from His example? What does it mean for us that His victory on the cross broke Satan's power over us? How does the power of Jesus' resurrection become a tool for us when we're tempted?

Closing

Divide youth into pairs. Assign a technique from the Team Page Teamwork Part B. Have teams model how "risk escape" might be done. One youth will try to "tempt" the other into a risky situation. The second youth uses the technique to get away.

Close with prayer asking for guidance, support, and wisdom when making choices.

Teamwork Part A

Bible Reflection:
Been There, Done That

Read about Jesus' temptations in the following passage. Discuss modern-day temptations that parallel the temptations of Jesus. How did Christ handle it? Is there anything we can learn from His example? What does it mean for us that His victory on the cross broke Satan's power over us? How does the power of Jesus' resurrection become a tool for us when we're tempted?

Then Jesus was led up by the Spirit into the wilderness to be tempted by the devil. He fasted forty days and forty nights, and afterwards he was famished. The tempter came and said to him, "If you are the Son of God, command these stones to become loaves of bread." But he answered, "It is written, 'One does not live by bread alone, but by every word that comes from the mouth of God.'" Then the devil took him to the holy city and placed him on the pinnacle of the temple, saying to him, "If you are the Son of God, throw yourself down; for it is written, 'He will command his angels concerning you,' and 'On their hands they will bear you up, so that you will not dash your foot against a stone.'" Jesus said to him, "Again it is written, 'Do not put the Lord your God to the test.'" Again, the devil took him to a very high mountain and showed him all the kingdoms of the world and their splendor; and he said to him, "All these I will give you, if you will fall down and worship me." Jesus said to him, "Away with you, Satan! for it is written, 'Worship the Lord your God, and serve only him.'" (Matthew 4:1–10 NRSV)

Teamwork Part B

Closing

Together with a friend, identify a risky behavior, choose a technique from the list below, and practice how it might be used while one of you tries to "tempt" the other into the risky situation.
Practice makes perfect. Switch roles and do it again.

- Be assertive. Say no. No explanation from you is necessary.

- Act shocked: "You know I would never choose to do that!"

- Walk away. Act distracted, like you didn't even hear them.

- Kiss up: "I know you are way too smart to try that."

- Make an excuse: "I've got to be home by …"

- Make it into a joke: "Like I'm really going to do this and be grounded for the rest of my life."

- Remind them of someone they look down upon who did a similar thing.

- Say you are not feeling up to it.

10A

Scripture: © NRSV. © 1999 CPH   **Team Page** *What's Happening?*

Going to the youth group at your church	Copying homework	Smoking cigarettes
Trying marijuana	Reporting vandalism	"Borrowing" your older brother or sister's stuff without asking
Going to the beach	Lying to your parents	Sneaking out of the house at night
Joining an athletic team	Telling on a friend who is doing drugs	Telling an embarrassing story about someone
Lying to a friend	Going shopping	Going to the movies
Skipping school	Kissing	Cheating
Flirting with girls/guys	Cussing at a teacher	Talking back to a teacher
Being in the bedroom of a girl or guy when no adults are around	Attempting to "go all the way" sexually	Whispering in class

10B Team Page *Cards for This and That Warm-Up Activity* © 1999 CPH

Values Check

Identifying Values

11

Introduction

This session will introduce the importance of values and their effect on behavior. The youth will see values as the underlying motivational factors when people choose behaviors and actions. A better understanding of their own values will help them to understand and hopefully accept others with different values.

Key Concept

Youth will see values and behavior as interrelated.

Goals

Youth will identify their own values and learn how values shape behavioral choices. By comparing their values with others, they will learn to understand and accept personal differences.

Bible Reference

Paul before and after his conversion (Acts 9:1–4; 13:42–48)

Presession

Using old magazine pictures, yarn, and hangers, have students make a mobile of the most valuable things in life. Just before class begins, have them hang their mobile and explain it to the rest of the class.

Lesson Overview

Activity	Summary	Goal	Materials	Time
Presession	Create a mobile of priorities	Identify what is of value	Hangers, yarn, scissors, magazines	First arrival to start of session
Warm-up	Values Check card game	Introduce value words	One card deck (master provided) for every six players	20 minutes
Focus	Choose a value	Rank your values and receive feedback from others	Team Page, pencils	20 minutes
Activity	What's My Line?	Guess the mystery value	Team Page, three blindfolds	15 minutes
Bible Reflection	Acts 9:1–4 and Acts 13:42–48 (Paul before and after his conversion)	See how life in Christ shapes our values and changes our lives	Bibles	15 minutes
Closing	Prayer stems	Youth pray in a group	Team Page	5 minutes

Warm-Up: Values-Check Card Game

Divide the youth into teams of six people (five if necessary). Give them a deck of cards from the reproducible page in this lesson. Each deck should include six values (honesty, justice, knowledge, love, loyalty, truth), with four cards representing each value, plus the three miscellaneous cards. Have each group shuffle and deal all the cards to the participants. Three players will receive an extra card.

Players try to collect one complete set of four identical cards or its equivalent using wild cards. This is done by trading with others in the group. Each player determines the value of the cards they are willing to trade, calling out how many cards they are willing to trade. Players can only trade with people who are trading for the same number of cards. In other words, a person who wants to trade three cards must trade with another person trading three cards, and so on. The Peter and Mary cards are wild. As soon as a person has collected four of the same cards (or its equivalent using wild cards), they announce it to the group by saying, "Values Check!" and lay down their hand. The other players lay down their cards, and points are tabulated. Players receive 25 points for a pair that matches, 50 points for three of a kind, or 100 points for four of a kind. Whoever is holding the devil card at the end receives no points. Play a few rounds.

Discuss: What made you decide the value of each card? What other things do we value? How do we identify our values?

Focus: Choose a Value

Say, **Today we are going to explore the importance of values. Values are a major part of what we believe and how we behave. Our values influence our behavior. Values help us determine our priorities, organize our time, and evaluate ourselves. They also help us to determine our goals in life.** Hand out the Team Page. **On the Team Page you will see some values listed on the left. Choose your top 10 values and rank them from most important to least important.** Give the youth time to fill in their numbers on the Team Page. Invite them to share their answers.

The second column is for the values you want to have. Rank these as you did in the first column. Allow them time to do this. Ask them to compare their ranking in both columns. Invite them to share their observations and some possible reasons for the differences.

You are going to give your list to a friend in this group. Please rate the other person on what you think their real values are, based on their behavior. Have them exchange their value chart with a friend and fill in the third column with the same kind of ranking based on their observable behaviors. Have students return the papers and discuss the content. Encourage them to be honest in their assessments and share their learnings.

Our values motivate us. They are the "wind in our sail" that empowers our behavior. This values chart reminds you of their importance and how our values may be perceived by others. How might it be a challenge to get to know someone who has different values than you have? Discuss responses.

Activity: What's My Line?

Three youth are chosen to be contestants. They are blindfolded.

A host describes one of the values on the Team Page list without specifically naming it.

The three contestants can only ask "yes or no" questions until they think they know the value. The contestant who correctly guesses is the winner.

Bible Reflection

Look at the following verses in the Bible and discuss which of St. Paul's values may have changed.

Before his conversion: Acts 9:1–4
After his conversion: Acts 13:42–48

How does the power of Jesus Christ also change our values through the work of the Holy Spirit? What does it mean for us to live with the values of a Christian?

Closing

End with a prayer in which each youth reads the prayer from the Team Page.

Other Resources

Old Turtle, text by Douglas Wood, watercolors by Cheng-Khee Chee (Pfeifer Hamilton Publishers, 210 West Michigan, Duluth, Minnesota 55802; phone: 218-727-0500)

Teamwork *Values Evaluation*

VALUE CHOICES Rank your TOP 10.	This is me!	This is how I want to be!	This is how my friend sees me!
Wisdom (Good Sense)			
Wealth			
Faith (Relationship with God)			
Fun (Joy, Pleasure)			
Power			
Popularity			
Loyalty			
Love			
Knowledge (Seeking Truth)			
Service (Doing for Others)			
Honesty			
Emotional Well-Being			
Creativity (Being Original)			
Independence (Making My Own Decisions)			
Achievement (Success)			
Humor			

Prayer Finish this sentence.

Thank You, God, for adding the value of

_____ to my life.

It helps me to _____

_____ .

Honesty	Honesty	Honesty	Honesty
Justice	Justice	Justice	Justice
Knowledge	Knowledge	Knowledge	Knowledge
Love	Love	Love	Love
Loyalty	Loyalty	Loyalty	Loyalty
Truth	Truth	Truth	Truth
Devil	Peter-wild	Mary-wild	Copy makes one deck. (Make one deck for every six people.)

11B

Listening, the Language of Friends

The Skill of Parroting

12

Introduction

Psychologist Carl Rogers said, "When I say that I enjoy hearing some-one, I mean, of course, hearing deeply. I mean that I hear the words, the thoughts, the feelings, the tones, the personal meaning, even the meaning that is below the conscious intent of the speaker." Listening deeply sends a message that you care about the person. This lesson will give participants an opportunity to practice the art of listening carefully to someone.

Key Concept

Listening is more than hearing. Listening is an attempt to hear the whole person. This important friendship skill takes practice.

Goals

Participants will practice four different listening exercises. They will celebrate with the psalmist that God listens to them and answers their prayer.

Bible Reference

Psalm 86

Presession

Prepare a tape recording of 10 different noises. Be sure to leave 10 to 15 second pauses between each sound. As the youth arrive, invite them to

Lesson Overview

Activity	Summary	Goal	Materials	Time
Presession	Listen for the sounds	To introduce the idea of listening carefully	Cassette (recorded beforehand), tape recorder	Before class time
Warm-up	Remember people's names	To teach the importance of learning people's names and remembering what they say	None	20 minutes
Focus	Telephone game	To show that careful listening is more than words	Newsprint or chalkboard, writing implement	10 minutes
Activity	Now Hear This game	To practice parroting as a listening technique	Team Page, game cards (printed beforehand)	20 minutes
Bible Reflection	Listening to God's voice in Scripture	Paraphrasing familiar passages	Note cards with Bible references, Bibles	10 minutes
Closing	Psalm 86	Responsive prayer	Team Page	3 minutes

play the recording and identify the sounds. Possible sounds to record might be a car horn, dropping a fork, crumpling paper, flushing a toilet, typing on a keyboard, scratching a book cover, an alarm clock buzzer, radio static, using a light switch, using a microwave oven, and paper clips falling onto a desk.

Warm-Up

Welcome everyone and announce that this lesson will help them discover how well they listen. Play the tape-recorded sounds one last time, having them guess each sound. Share the correct answers.

Explain the Name Add-on game. **Take a moment to think of a feeling that describes you today that begins with the first letter of your first name. Like Sally-Sad or Emily-Excited. We will go around the room and have you share your name and the feeling word. When it is your turn, please say the name and feeling word of each person who has gone before you—in order—before sharing your name and word. The last person will end up saying everyone's name and feeling word.**

Focus: Telephone Wire

Say, **Have you ever played the Telephone game? I will whisper a sentence to one person, and they will pass it around the circle until it comes back to me. The last person repeats the message out loud and we will see if it is still the same.**

Here is a possible message: **Mark is going on vacation to Chicago with his family and his best friend, Pete. He hopes the trip won't ruin their relationship.**

Write what the last person says on newsprint or a chalkboard to compare with the original message. Ask, **Who might be hoping it won't ruin the relationship? Which relationship might it be?** Say, **Listening to words alone may not tell the whole message.**

Activity: Now Hear This—Parroting

Ask, **Have you ever listened to an airplane pilot talk to the airport control tower?** Say, **Air traffic controllers and many other radio operators utilize a method of communication called parroting. The controller might say, "Delta flight 1000, you are clear to taxi to runway 4 westbound." The pilot**

then repeats the information back to the controller saying, **"Roger, Delta 1000 taxiing to runway 4 westbound." The repetition of the information completes the loop and increases the accuracy of communication. This way of listening also works for friends who want to communicate better with each other.**

Prepare a set of cards for each group using the reproducible page at the end of the unit. Tell the youth to form groups of three and decide who will play each role. Announce that you will put a stack of cards in the center of each triad. Person 1 is to pick up the card and read it silently and carefully. Person 1 will then say the words to Person 2 in a way that expresses feelings. Person 2 will repeat the phrase back to Person 1. Person 3 will decide if Person 2 heard the most important parts of the message and repeated it back correctly. Person 3 assigns zero points for a complete miscommunication, one point for most of the message, and three points for all the important parts. Students don't have to say it exactly word for word, but for three points they need to repeat all the information. Rotate roles each time.

Ask for two volunteers and demonstrate the three steps of the exercise. Make sure everyone has a Team Page and a set of the cards. There are nine cards, for three rounds each.

Bible Reflection: Parroting God's Word

Make at least one index card for each student with one of the following Bible references written on one side: John 3:16; Ephesians 2:8–9; Romans 8:28; Romans 8:38–39; Isaiah 40:28–31; Jeremiah 29:11–14; Colossians 3:12–17; Ephesians 6:10–18; Psalm 23; Matthew 28:16–20; John 15:9–17. Use as many different references as possible. Distribute cards to students, and have them read the passage first, then "parrot" what God is saying by writing their meaning on the other side of the index card in their own words. Have some of the students share their answers. Ask, **How does God show He loves us in these words? How important is it that we know His love?**

Closing

Use the Team Page and prepare the groups to read their parts responsively.

Now Hear This Game

Step A—Get in groups of three.

Step B—Assign each person either role 1, role 2, or role 3.

Step C—Person 1 takes a card, reads it silently, and repeats it, attempting to communicate feelings.

Step D—Person 2 repeats the information back to Person 1, covering all the important points.

Step E—Person 3 judges how well Person 2 did and records the score below.

Responsive Prayer

Leader: Our prayer is from the Bible, where the psalmist writes:

Everyone: Incline your ear, O LORD, and answer me, for I am poor and needy.

Boys: Preserve my life, for I am devoted to you; save your servant who trusts in you. You are my God;

Girls: Be gracious to me, O Lord, for to you do I cry all day long. Gladden the soul of your servant, for to you, O Lord, I lift up my soul.

Leader: For you, O Lord, are good and forgiving, abounding in steadfast love to all who call on you.

Everybody: Give ear, O LORD, to my prayer; listen to my cry of supplication. In the day of my trouble I call on you, for you will answer me.

Boys: There is none like you among the gods, O Lord, nor are there any works like yours.

Girls: All the nations you have made shall come and bow down before you, O Lord, and shall glorify your name. For you are great and do wondrous things; you alone are God.

Everyone: Teach me your way, O LORD, that I may walk in your truth; give me an undivided heart to revere your name. I give thanks to you, O Lord God, with my whole heart, and I will glorify your name forever.

Leader: This is Psalm 86.

Everyone: Amen.

My Listening—Repeating Score	
Round One	
Round Two	
Round Three	
Total Score	

Scripture: © NRSV. © 1999 CPH

I have been so unhappy with my new school. Everyone seems so stuck up. No one likes the kind of music I listen to. I feel like I am suffocating.

I can't wait until the end of this year. I have so many great things planned for this summer. Our vacation will be the best. I wish I could take my best friend. But I don't think the dates will work out.

I wish my biology teacher would back off with the homework. I spend as much time on the biology assignment as I do on all the others combined. Everyone in the class is complaining, but no one wants to say anything to the teacher. I told my mom, and she said to wait and see if I get used to it. I would rather get out of the class.

Wow, this is the greatest year of my life so far. My grades are up. I love all my teachers. I have the best friends ever. Best of all, my parents are letting me go to the concert next Friday.

Have you heard the latest news? There aren't going to be any athletics next year because of cutbacks in the budget. I think that will really ruin school spirit.

I am just interested in him as a friend, yet everyone thinks we should go out. I wish people would mind their own business. It is none of their concern if I like somebody for a friend or if I want to go out with him.

I need someone to listen to me. I have this great opportunity to be in a band, but it will take a lot of money for the new amplifier. I have been trying to make a decision, but I need the perfect time to bring it up with my parents.

I don't get it. One minute Tim and Dawn act like I'm their best friend, and the next minute they act like they don't want to be seen with me. I am beginning to think I did something to upset them, but I don't know what it is.

I'm afraid to go home. My mom says as soon as I get home we will go to the hospital and see my grandma. I hate hospitals—they smell—and I hate to see grandma so sick without being able to do anything. She might die soon, though.

12B

Team Page *Cards for the "Now Hear This" Game*

Listen for Feelings
The Key to Peer Relationships

Introduction

Listening to and focusing on the feelings of others is the key to effective peer relationships. The first step involves becoming aware of our own feelings.

Key Concept

Feelings are a wonderful gift from God. We can learn to accept and appreciate our feelings and the feelings of others. Expressing our feelings helps build relationships. Listening for others' feelings has been called "active" listening.

Goals

The participants will
- Learn that human feelings are an important gift from God.
- Learn to recognize and identify the feelings of others.
- Learn that expressing both positive and negative feelings leads to closer and more authentic relationships.
- Listen for feelings in others.

Bible Reference

St. Paul shares his feelings about the people of Philippi (Philippians 1:1–9).

Lesson Overview

Activity	Summary	Goal	Materials	Time
Presession	Examination of mystery boxes and mood pictures	Youth learn to feel with their fingers and with their heart	Mystery box and items, clean socks, magazines	First arrival to starting time
Warm-up	Explore what today "felt" like	Begin stating feelings	8½" × 11" paper, marking pens	10 minutes
Focus	Expressing feelings	Teach the difference between thinking and feeling	None	5 minutes
Activity	Brainstorm "feelings" vocabulary	Help youth use words to express feelings	Newsprint or chalkboard, writing implement	10 minutes
Bible Reflection	Finding feelings in St. Paul's letter, listening to each other	Students practice looking for feelings under the surface of words	Team Page, pencils	20 minutes
Closing	Circle evaluation and reading	Students demonstrate active listening	Lesson plan	5 minutes

Presession

Prepare two or three "mystery boxes" by placing a combination of objects with unique or interesting textures (pine cone, coral, shell, a potato, foil, etc.) inside a box. Cut a hole in the side large enough for someone to reach in. Glue or staple the top of a sock around the opening so participants can stick their hand into the box through the sock, touching the items without seeing inside. Invite each participant to reach into the mystery boxes and describe what they "feel" like.

Distribute an extra clean sock to each student. Have them close their eyes, put their hand into the sock, and imagine that they are feeling each of these emotions: anger, love, peace, despair, hope, joy. Have them describe what they "feel."

Distribute magazines. Have students select a picture of a person. Have them show the picture to the group and share what they believe the person in the picture might be feeling.

Warm-Up

Bring everyone together and say, **Welcome everyone. How are you feeling today? (Pause.) Perhaps a better question is, "What are you feeling today?" Today we are going to explore the idea that our emotions are a wonderful gift from God. We are going to practice sharing our feelings and listening for the feelings of others. We will see how listening for feelings and not judging them is a great way to communicate with each other.**

Give each person an 8½" × 11" paper and a marking pen. Ask them to draw a picture or write a word or short phrase that describes one feeling they have had today.

Have participants form groups by finding others who shared the same or a related feeling on their paper. Point out that the basic feelings of anger, joy, sadness, and fear have many different tones and intensities. Further combine groups into basic feelings groups and discuss what this means.

Focus

Ask the group to be seated where they can all see and hear you. Write "I feel that ..." on a chalkboard or newsprint. Discuss how the word "that" changes the message from a feeling to a thought.

Example: I feel satisfied. (Feeling)

I feel that things are going well. (Thought)

Say, **In this unit you will be sharing feelings in your small groups. Feelings are a gift to be shared. Even uncomfortable feelings help us better understand each other. Practice describing your feelings and learn to accept the feelings of others.**

Activity: Brainstorm "Feeling" Words

Tell the group that you would like to build a vocabulary of "feeling" words. Go to the chalkboard or newsprint and write all the words they tell you. If it is not a true "feeling" word, listen and help them describe the feeling behind the word. Include slang words. Ask them to help you understand the feelings behind the words.

Bible Reflection: Team Page

Divide into groups of four or five youth by having each person stand in a line according to birth dates and breaking it up from there. You will need copies of Teamwork Part A of the Team Page and pencils. Have each group select a leader and identify someone who will pick up the materials. Allow 20 minutes for discussion.

Tell them to use the list on the Team Page and the one they just brainstormed to describe the feelings of St. Paul in Teamwork Part A. Encourage and help them as they work on the assignment.

When you see that most have finished part A, distribute the "Listen for Feelings" cartoon and briefly describe what it is depicting. Do Teamwork Part B in pairs. If there are uneven groups, you can have some threesomes.

Closing

Gather the group into a circle and ask for any comments or evaluations of the session's activities. Listen to the comments without defending or objecting to what they say. Close with the following blessing:

Hear the words of St. Paul to you today: "I thank my God every time I remember you, constantly praying with every one of my prayers for all of you, because of your sharing the gospel from the first day until now. I am confident of this, that the one who began a good work among you will bring it to completion" (Philippians 1:3–6).

Teamwork Part A

It is important to tell our friends how we think and how we feel. Sharing thoughts and feelings is an essential communication skill for healthy relationships. In general, thinking words ("head talk") explain a situation, while feeling words ("gut talk") help us better understand a situation.

The adjoining greeting from St. Paul has been divided up into several phrases. Look at each phrase and discuss what his feelings might be.

Paul and Timothy, servants of Christ Jesus, To all the saints in Christ Jesus who are in Philippi, with the bishops and deacons: Grace to you and peace from God our Father and the Lord Jesus Christ.

Feelings: _____

I thank my God every time I remember you, constantly praying with joy in every one of my prayers for all of you, because of your sharing in the gospel from the first day until now.

Feelings: _____

I am confident of this, that the one who began a good work among you will bring it to completion by the day of Jesus Christ.

Feelings: _____

It is right for me to think this way about all of you, because you hold me in your heart, for all of you share in God's grace with me, both in my imprisonment and in the defense and confirmation of the gospel.

Feelings: _____

For God is my witness, how I long for all of you with the compassion of Christ Jesus. (Philippians 1:1–9 NRSV)

Feelings: _____

"Feeling" Words

Happy	Anger
content	aggravated
curious	annoyed
playful	frustrated
relaxed	furious
interested	hurt
confident	resentful

Sad	Fear
alone	scared
anxious	shocked
discouraged	shy
helpless	skeptical
lonely	worried
	terrified

Teamwork Part B

Divide into pairs. Using the "Listen for Feelings" handout, each pair will practice expressing feelings and sharing with each other at a deeper level. Avoid expressing thoughts (don't use the word "that"); attempt to share genuine feelings.

1. When I am away from my family, I feel …
2. When I fail at something, I feel …
3. When there is an argument, I feel …
4. Right now I am feeling …

A Prayer (with Feeling)

Dear heavenly Father, we thank You for creating us with emotions. Help us to see them as wonderful gifts of life. Help us use them to better understand one another. Remind us that Your Holy Spirit understands our feelings and our sighs too deep for words. In Jesus' name. Amen.

Although developing a sensitivity for feelings seems quite easy, it is important to practice and then use good listening skills.

SPEAKER
This person has lots of feelings and expresses them with words.

LISTENER
This person attempts to listen by asking what he thinks she is feeling.

Practice listening to each other.

Step One: Find a partner.

Step Two: Flip a coin to decide who will speak and who will listen.

Step Three: The speaker shares something important going on in his or her life. The listener tries to guess the feeling. (Go for three minutes.)

Step Four: The speaker gives some feedback to the listener on how well he/she listened.

Last Step: Switch roles and follow steps three and four.

Team Page *Listen for Feelings Handout*

Iceberg Feelings

Identifying Hidden Feelings

Introduction

Feelings have been described as being like an iceberg. There can be one strong feeling expressed (above the surface of the water), while many other contributing feelings still lie beneath the surface. Caring friends recognize that the surface feelings may only be the tip of the iceberg and that additional care and listening will help uncover other feelings.

Key Concept

Feelings are complex. The first feeling that is expressed may mask many different or even conflicting feelings.

Goals

The youth will reflect upon their feelings during a simulation. They will explore the different feelings of the prodigal son and waiting father in the parable. This lesson will encourage them to accept feelings as God's gift to people.

Bible Reference

The parable of the forgiving father (Luke 15:11–32 NRSV)

Presession: Sign In

Cover a large wall with newsprint. As the youth arrive, have them write down their name and some of their feelings from the past week. Draw a circle around the most common feeling recorded.

Lesson Overview

Activity	Summary	Goal	Materials	Time
Presession	Create a list of feelings	Introduce the topic and create atmosphere	Newsprint, marking pens	First arrival to beginning
Warm-up	Balloon relay	Warm up group and introduce the game	Balloons and three chairs	15 minutes
Focus	Iceberg theory	Teach how feelings are often layered	Newsprint or chalkboard	10 minutes
Activity	Balloon relay with simulation	Create different feelings and discuss them	Balloons, three chairs, Team Page, pencils	30 minutes
Bible Reflection	The story of the forgiving father	Explore the son's feelings	Team Page, pencils	15 minutes
Closing	Psalm 130	Use a prayer expressing deep feelings	Team Page	5 minutes

Warm-Up: Balloon Relay

Divide the group into three teams and distribute one balloon to each person. Create a starting point behind which each relay team stands in line. Place a chair for each team about 30 feet away. In turn, each person on the team must blow up a balloon, run to the chair, sit on the balloon until it pops, and return to the starting point. The relay will be run again during the Activity.

Focus: Iceberg Theory

Draw an iceberg on newsprint or a chalkboard (see below). Explain how one expressed feeling may often hide additional and more "risky" feelings kept under the surface. Ask for examples.

Activity: Simulation

Make sure that you arrange before the session to have a youth fake a loud protest of complaint when prizes are unfairly awarded after this second round of the relay. Announce to the class that the relay will be repeated, but this time there will be prizes. Run the race;

award the first-place team a single tiny candy from a bag; award the second-place team a small single candy; award each member of the losing team with a full candy bar. When the designated youth begins complaining loudly, send him or her from the room, saying, **Well, if you don't like my prizes, you can stand in the hallway for five minutes.** Forcefully move the student outside; close the door. After 15 seconds or so, allow the student to return. Reveal that it was arranged beforehand.

Distribute the Team Page Handout and have students complete the Teamwork Part A graph independently. Allow time to complete the grid; then form groups of four or five to complete the question under the grid.

Bible Reflection

Have students stay in their groups to complete Teamwork Part B, about the prodigal son and the forgiving father.

Closing: Forgiveness

Pray the prayer from the Team Page.

Teamwork Part A

Write down your feelings as you remember experiencing them during the balloon relay race that just occurred.

What happened ...	What were you feeling?	What were you doing?
During the relay game		
When prizes were given		
When the youth started acting up		
When the youth was kicked out		
When you found out it was an act		

Prayer for Forgiveness

Out of the depths I cry to you, O LORD. Lord, hear my voice! Let your ears be attentive to the voice of my supplications! If you, O LORD, should mark iniquities, Lord, who could stand? But there is forgiveness with you, so that you may be revered. I wait for the LORD, my soul waits, and in his word I hope; my soul waits for the LORD more than those who watch for the morning, more than those who watch for the morning. O Israel, hope in the LORD! For with the LORD there is steadfast love, and with him is great power to redeem. It is he who will redeem Israel from all its iniquities. (Psalm 130 NRSV)

God truly knows and understands all of our feelings. We rejoice that we can honestly share with Him and know that He accepts us.

Discuss your feelings and actions with your group. What actions were appropriate and what actions were inappropriate? Feelings happen; how we act upon our feelings is important.

14A

Team Page *Iceberg Feelings*

Teamwork Part B

Read the following Bible story and underline the feelings of the younger son. Then write them on the iceberg below.

Then Jesus said, "There was a man who had two sons. The younger of them said to his father, 'Father, give me the share of the property that will belong to me.' So he divided his property between them. A few days later the younger son gathered all he had and traveled to a distant country, and there he squandered his property in dissolute living. When he had spent everything, a severe famine took place throughout that country, and he began to be in need. So he went and hired himself out to one of the citizens of that country, who sent him to his fields to feed the pigs. He would gladly have filled himself with the pods that the pigs were eating: and no one gave him anything. But when he came to himself he said, 'How many of my father's hired hands have bread enough and to spare, but here I am dying of hunger! I will get up and go to my father, and I will say to him, "Father, I have sinned against heaven and before you; I am no longer worthy to be called your son; treat me like one of your hired hands." ' So he set off and went to his father. But while he was still far off, his father saw him and was filled with compassion; he ran and put his arms around him and kissed him. Then the son said to him, 'Father, I have sinned against heaven and before you; I am no longer worthy to be called your son.' But the father said to his slaves, 'Quickly, bring out a robe—the best one—and put it on him; put a ring on his finger and sandals on his feet. And get the fatted calf and kill it, and let us eat and celebrate; for this son of mine was dead and is alive again; he was lost and is found!' And they began to celebrate." (Luke 15:11–24 NRSV)

How do you feel knowing that God's love for you is like that of the waiting father, welcoming, accepting, and restoring us when we've failed Him? What does it mean to live in God's forgiveness and love? How does God show us this kind of love?

Iceberg Theory.

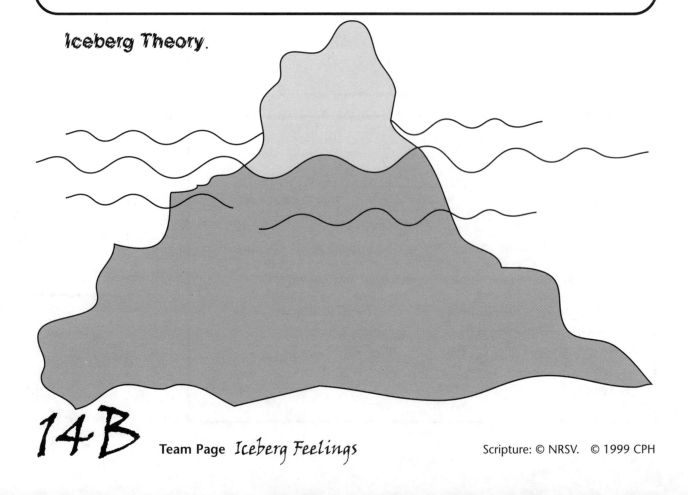

14B

Team Page *Iceberg Feelings*

I Can Feel Your Pain

Empathy

Introduction

We can learn how to be more empathetic. This lesson is a step in the process. Empathy is an important part of communication. Empathy is the ability to "walk in another person's shoes," working hard to understand someone else's feelings, thoughts, and motives—both those on the surface and those underneath. To empathize is to hear and understand another person accurately. In *Peer Power*, author Dr. Judith A. Tindall says, "Empathy involves experiencing another's world as if you were they."

Key Concept

Youth will recognize the skill of empathy and begin to apply this skill.

Goals

Youth will practice and utilize the skill of empathy.

Bible Reference

Matthew 9:36

Presession: Movie Critics

Create a movie mural from a variety of current newspaper and magazine movie advertisements and reviews, leaving space for student comments. Label it "Movie Critics." Invite students to write their own review of the movies they've seen, signing their names. Have them also list all the feelings the movie created in them when they watched it.

Lesson Overview

Activity	Summary	Goal	Materials	Time
Presession	Movie critics	Explore the feelings people get from films	Mural paper, glue, marking pens, movie advertisements	Before class begins
Warm-up	Speaking with feelings	Listening for feelings in the Bible passage	Bible	10 minutes
Focus	Introduce the theme	Teaching the art of paraphrasing and parroting	Teachers Guide, lemon, knife	10 minutes
Activity	Chat Room interaction	Practice writing listening responses	Team Page, pencils	15 minutes
Bible Reflection	Matthew 9:36	Identify people who need compassion and make a plan to provide it	Team Page	5 minutes
Closing	Commitment	Youth consider who they might listen to in the coming week	Team Page	10 minutes

Warm-Up: Say It with Feeling

Read the following passage:

When they had finished breakfast, Jesus said to Simon Peter, "Simon son of John, do you love me more than these?" He said to him, "Yes, Lord; you know that I love you." Jesus said to him, "Feed my lambs." A second time he said to him, "Simon son of John, do you love me?" He said to him, "Yes, Lord; you know that I love you." Jesus said to him, "Tend my sheep." He said to him the third time, "Simon son of John, do you love me?" Peter felt hurt because he said to him the third time, "Do you love me?" And he said to him, "Lord, you know everything; you know that I love you." Jesus said to him, "Feed my sheep. Very truly, I tell you, when you were younger, you used to fasten your own belt and to go wherever you wished. But when you grow old, you will stretch out your hands, and someone else will fasten a belt around you and take you where you do not wish to go." (John 21:15–18 NRSV)

After the reading, ask

What feelings did you hear in Jesus' words?
What feelings did you hear in Peter's words?
What might have prompted this type of statement?
How might Peter clarify his feelings?
What might you feel if Jesus came to you with the same good news?

Focus: Listen with Empathy

Illustrate empathy by asking the youth to closely watch your movements. Take a lemon and cut it into wedges. Slowly and dramatically, bring one of the wedges to your mouth and take a bite. Watch the responses of the youth and ask how many found they were able to imagine the taste of the lemon enough to begin salivating.

Say, **Many of you began to salivate when watching me taste this lemon. You were "with me" enough to physically have the same response I had. That is a type of empathy. Empathy is a skill that we can get better at. Many times our own agenda gets in the way when we try to understand another person. In order to foster meaningful communi-** cation, we must strive to put our own thoughts and feelings aside and focus totally on the other person. We try to understand the other person so completely that their surface and deeper thoughts, motives, and feelings become apparent to us.

One way to listen with empathy is to repeat back to someone what you think you heard them say. This is known as "parroting," that is, repeating to the speaker almost exactly what they have said. Another form is "paraphrasing," which is repeating the essence of what you heard them say in your own words. Using either one of these responses allows the speaker to know that they have been heard accurately. It also allows them to reflect on the thoughts and feelings they are expressing.

Activity: The Chat Room

Divide the youth into groups of three. One person is the sender or speaker. Another is the listener. These two people go to different parts of the room, while the third person becomes the "cyber guy." The cyber guy is to deliver the messages between the two others much like e-mail over the Internet. Have the first person write a message with feelings on the Team Page, Teamwork Part A. The cyber guy delivers this page to the other person. The receiver writes a listening response (either parroting or paraphrasing) and sends it back again. After about three or four exchanges, start over with a new copy of the Team Page, rotating the role of each person. Repeat the activity one more time, to ensure that each person experiences each role. Have youth share examples of good empathetic responses with the group.

Bible Reflection: Team Page

"When he saw the crowds, he had compassion for them, because they were harassed and helpless, like sheep without a shepherd" (Matthew 9:36 NRSV). Discuss the questions on the Team Page, Teamwork Part B.

Closing: Team Page

Turn to the Team Page. Have students think of a possible situation where they could use empathetic listening in the coming week. They should share the potential situation with their group.

Teamwork Part A

Empathy combines open-ended questions, listening for feelings, and interpreting body language. This skill helps the listener to understand the speaker's surface feelings and explore their deeper feelings, thoughts, and motives.

E-Mail Message   Screen Name: _____

My thoughts and feelings about the first day of school are:

_____

Listening Response: _____

_____

What I like best about church: _____

_____

Listening Response: _____

_____

The thing that bothers me most about my friends:

_____

_____

Listening Response: _____

_____

One way to listen with empathy is to repeat back to someone what you think you heard them say. This is known as "parroting," that is, repeating to the speaker almost exactly what they have said. Another form is "paraphrasing," which is repeating the essence of what you heard them say in your own words. Using either one of these responses allows the speaker to know that they have been heard accurately. It also allows them to reflect on the thoughts and feelings they are expressing.

Teamwork Part B

Read this passage about Jesus.

"When he saw the crowds, he had compassion for them, because they were harassed and helpless, like sheep without a shepherd" (Matthew 9:36 NRSV).

When do we especially need Jesus as our Shepherd? Do you know anybody else who needs a shepherd like Jesus?

Closing

Think of a possible situation where you might use empathetic listening in the coming week.

Share that with your group.

16 I See What You Are Thinking

Nonverbal Communication

Introduction

Communicating involves more than just speaking and listening to words. Only 5 percent of a spoken message depends upon the actual words used. 80 percent of interpersonal communication is nonverbal, and 15 percent of communication is shaped by the manner in which something is said. This awareness will help youth listen more completely and be better peer counselors.

Key Concept

Youth learn to pay attention to nonverbal aspects of communication.

Goals

Youth will learn to pay attention to nonverbal body language in their messages and the messages of others.

Lesson Overview

Activity	Summary	Goal	Materials	Time
Presession	Video and music expression	Youth express themselves nonverbally	Video camera, VCR, and TV; or CDs and CD player	Before class
Warm-up	Expression match	Youth identify expressions in pictures	Old magazines, scissors, paste, poster board, marking pens	20 minutes
Focus	Nonverbal messages	Teach how to read the meaning of body language and tone	Chalkboard and chalk, or newsprint and marking pens	5 minutes
Activity	Body language charades	Youth identify thoughts and feelings from body language	Charade cards, timer	20 minutes
Bible Reflection	Imagine Bible character body language	Students project real emotions onto the biblical record	Team Page, pencils	10 minutes
Closing	Video	Celebrate each person in the group as a gift from God	TV/VCR	10 minutes

Bible Reference

Stories where Jesus reveals some emotion:
- Jesus blessing the children (Matthew 19:13–15)
- Jesus and the large catch of fish (Luke 5:3–8)
- Jesus walks on water (Matthew 14:23–29)

Presession: Show Your Feelings

Play short samples of different music representing a variety of moods and feelings. Have students discuss the nonverbal message of each selection.

Option One: Show Me Video

As each student arrives, use a video camera to tape them silently demonstrating different moods for the "Show Your Feelings" show. You may use a decorated background. Turn off the sound and watch the video segments, guessing emotions.

The camera operator may suggest feelings like embarrassment, anger, sadness, boredom, love, fear, joy, and others.

Be sure to stop the camera between expressions to keep it short and not give away the feeling.

Option Two: Sound Bites

Hand out suggested emotions from the list above and have each student select a sound bite from the CDs available that represents the assigned word.

Warm-Up: Mood Magazines

Write different feeling words in large letters along the top of poster board. Ask students to cut out magazine pictures depicting those feelings and paste them on the poster board.

Focus: Teaching about the Message

Write the following sentence on the chalkboard or newsprint: "I got sent home from school."

Ask, **How much do you know about this message by looking at the words?**

Write on the board:
Words—5%
Tone—15%
Body Language—80%
Explain that the words in a message only

convey 5 percent of the communication. The tone of voice adds 15 percent of the message, and the silent body language communicates the other 80 percent of the message. In order to really hear someone, it is important to watch them as well as listen to them.

Demonstrate by hanging your head in dejection, and with a sad face speak in somber tones, "I got sent home from school."

Now lift up your head, smile, and bounce on your toes, giving a high-five salute as you say with excitement, "I got sent home from school."

Discuss the differences. Allow students to communicate both expressions.

Activity: Charades

Divide into two groups to role-play the emotions from the charade cards (see Team Page 16B). One group takes a card and decides how to act it out. The other team is to guess the feelings being depicted. Have the groups alternate acting out the messages. Time each presentation and give a prize to the team that cumulatively takes less time to communicate their messages.

Bible Reflection: Team Page

Hand out the Team Page and ask the teams to look at the passages and imagine seeing the people in the story. What might they look like?

Closing: Celebrate Our Friends

Option One: Create a video of students as they arrive. Show the video, and when each person appears on the video the group shouts, "There's (name of youth). God loves you, (name of youth)."

Option Two: Have the youth stand in a circle. Ask one youth to be the expression leader. As you read Matthew 14:23–29, the leader will make expressions to match the reading and the entire group will imitate the expressions.

Other Resources

View the video "The Music Box," an award-winning allegory about a factory worker who finds a music box and discovers "hallelujah" in his "ho-hum" life. Distributed by White Lion Media. 20 minutes. Have the class try to identify the changing feelings of the main character.

Teamwork

For each story below, draw the mood of the people in their facial expression.

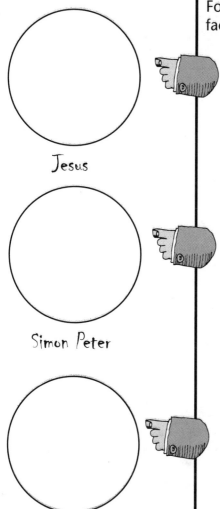

Jesus

Simon Peter

Disciples

Then little children were being brought to him in order that he might lay his hands on them and pray. The disciples spoke sternly to those who brought them; but Jesus said, "Let the little children come to me, and do not stop them; for it is to such as these that the kingdom of heaven belongs." And he laid his hands on them and went on his way. (Matthew 19:13–15 NRSV)

He got into one of the boats, the one belonging to Simon, and asked him to put out a little way from the shore. Then he sat down and taught the crowds from the boat. When he had finished speaking, he said to Simon, "Put out into the deep water and let down your nets for a catch." Simon answered, "Master, we have worked all night long but have caught nothing. Yet if you say so, I will let down the nets." When they had done this, they caught so many fish that their nets were beginning to break. So they signaled their partners in the other boat to come and help them. And they came and filled both boats, so that they began to sink. But when Simon Peter saw it, he fell down at Jesus' knees, saying, "Go away from me, Lord, for I am a sinful man!" (Luke 5:3–8 NRSV)

And after he had dismissed the crowds, he went up the mountain by himself to pray. When evening came, he was there alone, but by this time the boat, battered by the waves, was far from the land, for the wind was against them. And early in the morning he came walking toward them on the sea. But when the disciples saw him walking on the sea, they were terrified, saying, "It is a ghost!" And they cried out in fear. But immediately Jesus spoke to them and said, "Take heart, it is I; do not be afraid." Peter answered him, "Lord, if it is you, command me to come to you on the water." He said, "Come." So Peter got out of the boat, started walking on the water, and came toward Jesus. (Matthew 14:23–29 NRSV)

See the cartoons below.
What feeling might be communicated by each face?

"A picture is worth a thousand words."

16A

Team Page *I See What You Are Thinking*   Scripture: © NRSV.   ©1999 CPH

Intense
dislike
and anger

Amazement
and
disbelief

Disagreement
and
argument

Worry
and
fear
(about test results)

Boredom
and
apathy

Affection
and
love

17 What's Up?
The Art of Questioning

Introduction

Meeting new people and getting them to talk can be a real challenge. Even close acquaintances and friends may have difficulty talking about what is bothering them. This lesson focuses on helping students gain the skills to bridge the awkwardness of some situations.

Key Concept

The skill of asking questions.

Goals

To increase self-awareness about how our manner and choice of questions can either open up conversations or close them off.

Bible Reference

Luke 18:35–43

Presession

Post newsprint on one of the walls with the heading "My Questions for God" along the top. Have markers readily available for students to use as they arrive. Encourage everyone to put at least one question up; allow students to explain their question. Just before class begins, have the class select the first question they would like God to answer. Discuss briefly, **Why do you want God to answer these questions? How does the freedom to ask God questions affect your relationship with Him?**

Lesson Overview

Activity	Summary	Goal	Materials	Time
Presession	My questions for God	Students think about how important questions are to a relationship	Newsprint, markers	From first arrival until class begins
Warm-up	Asking closed questions	Open up group conversation	Index cards, pencils	10 minutes
Focus	Learning to draw out open and closed information	Youth will learn to use open questions in conversation	Two chairs in the center of the group	15 minutes
Activity	Youth ask open-ended questions	Youth will practice using open-ended questions	Team Page	10 minutes
Bible Reflection	Jesus' use of open-ended questions	Learning from Jesus' model	Team Page	10 minutes
Closing	Singing	Considering the questions we may have of God	Song "Here I Am Lord"	5 minutes

Warm-Up: Question Contest

Provide a large quantity of index cards and ask youth to get as many autographs from people in the group as they can. Under each autograph they should write the answers to the following questions:

- How old are you?
- Where were you born?
- What grade are you in?
- Where do you go to school?
- Do you like school?

When the youth have gathered at least five different cards with signatures and information, have them tell what they learned about the other person.

Focus: Open It/Close It

Say, **The questions you asked people and recorded on your cards are excellent examples of what are called "closed questions." They are closed because they do not allow the person much more than a one-word answer. Although this kind of factual information is needed some of the time, it does not allow us to really "know" who the person is or what they are like.**

Questions that allow additional information as answers are called "open-ended questions," because they give the speaker an opportunity to tell as much as he/she is comfortable sharing. Open-ended questions give more insight into how a person thinks, draw us closer together, and may help us share at a feelings level. Unless a person tells us what they are thinking and feeling, we can only guess what is going on with them.

Many open-ended questions start with the words "how" and "what." Instead of asking, "Who did this?" we might ask, "How was this done?" Instead of asking "Where were you born?" we could say, "What is your background?" or "Tell me about your background." Whenever someone gives an answer that's more than one word, you have an opportunity to get to know them better. Focusing on their feelings about a topic also allows the opportunity for the person to share more about themselves.

Demonstrate open/closed questions by interviewing a student volunteer. Allow others to review and evaluate.

Activity: Come On In!

Have the youth practice asking open-ended questions by dividing into two groups, lined up and facing each other but separated by a door or another barrier. Each member of the group outside will create an open-ended question to ask. When the door is opened, the questioner asks his/her question of the person inside facing them, and they respond. Each person who asks a true open-ended question is allowed to enter. If she asks a closed question, the door gets shut and she must go to the end of the line. When all have entered, the teams switch. (There might be snacks in the room as the reward for entering through the door.)

Have the youth explore the Team Page, Teamwork Part A, and individually choose the questions they believe are open-ended. Review the questions and discuss the answers, including ways for students to improve their use of open-ended questions.

Pair the youth with someone they do not know well. Instruct them to have one partner use three minutes to ask the least number of questions to keep the other talking the longest. Switch roles.

Discuss what made the exercise easy or difficult, and how it relates to everyday conversations.

Bible Reflection

Look at the Bible reference on the Team Page, Teamwork Part B (Luke 18:35–43). What are God's open-ended questions to us?

Closing

Think of an open-ended question you have for God. Take some time to ask Him during a personal prayer. Then as a group sing "Here I Am Lord."

Teamwork Part A

Closed questions ask for one-word answers that reveal little of how another person thinks or feels. Factual and informational questions often fall into this category.

Open-ended questions give the person opportunities to share more about themselves. They ask for opinions and feelings about topics. Many times words or phrases such as "Tell me about …" or "How did you …" or "What happened when …" are commonly used.

Which of the following questions are good open-ended questions?

1. Tell me about your math teacher.
2. How long did it take you to finish the assignment?
3. Do you go to math class every day?
4. What did you think about the exam?
5. Do you like skiing?
6. How do you feel about giving speeches?
7. Did you finish your homework?
8. What did you find hardest about the homework for today?
9. Do you yell when you get angry?
10. What do you do when you get angry?
11. Tell me why you reacted that way.
12. Were you upset?
13. Were you embarrassed when you dropped the tray?
14. What was going on when you dropped the tray?
15. You look stressed. What was your day like?
16. What are you going to do?

Teamwork Part B

Read the following passage. What are the open-ended questions in the account? What are some of God's open-ended questions to us? How is the forgiveness of Christ a closed statement about us? How does the freedom of the Gospel provide openness to the way we live our lives for Him?

Bible Reflection

As he approached Jericho, a blind man was sitting by the roadside begging. When he heard a crowd going by, he asked what was happening. They told him, "Jesus of Nazareth is passing by." Then he shouted, "Jesus, Son of David, have mercy on me!" Those who were in front sternly ordered him to be quiet; but he shouted even more loudly, "Son of David, have mercy on me!" Jesus stood still and ordered the man to be brought to him; and when he came near, he asked him, "What do you want me to do for you?" He said, "Lord, let me see again." Jesus said to him, "Receive your sight; your faith has saved you." Immediately he regained his sight and followed him, glorifying God; and all the people, when they saw it, praised God. (Luke 18:35–43 NRSV)

Keep Talking
Conversation Openers

Introduction

A listening response helps to keep the conversation going. Caring friends are able to listen in a way that helps people hear themselves and solve their own problems. Listening responses that focus on the listener rather than the speaker will stop the conversation.

Key Concept

It is an important life skill to help others express themselves by careful listening, reinforcing openers to conversation and discouraging conversation roadblocks.

Goals

Participants will determine which of two conversations is more helpful. They will practice listening responses and avoid roadblocks. They will examine what St. Paul has to say about caring for each other.

Bible Reference

Galatians 5:22–6:2

Presession: Fill in the Blanks

As youth arrive, ask each individual to provide a word or expression for at least one of the blanks in the story that follows. Do not read the story to the students at this time; read only the clues in parentheses. For the Warmup, you will read the entire story with the words they have given you. If you have enough youth, you can do the story twice with two sets of words.

Lesson Overview

Activity	Summary	Goal	Materials	Time
Presession	Fill in the blanks	Interact with others when they arrive	Story from Teachers Guide	Before class time
Warm-up	Group story	Read stories from Presession	Teachers Guide	10 minutes
Focus	Flash cards	Determine which response encourages speaking	Reproducible flash cards (provided)	10 minutes
Activity	Evaluating good listening responses	Choose the best listening response	Team Page	10 minutes
Bible Reflection	Exploring Galatians 5:22–6:2	Discovering the fruit of the Spirit	Team Page	10 minutes
Closing	Praying with prayer stems	Creating prayers of commitment and faith expression	Team Page	15 minutes

Troy was ready to go to school. He asked his Mom where his lunch was. She said (what you say when you are lost) _____. "Fine," said Troy, "I will just have to go to school without my (something in your room) _____." So he grabbed his (something in your garage) _____ and went out the door. As soon as he stepped into the sunlight, he knew this was going to be a (what you say when you are happy) _____ day. As he was headed for school, he noticed (girl's name) _____ coming from her house. He walked faster so he could (verb) _____ her. He said, "Hi," with a (animal) _____ in his throat. "Don't we look (color) _____ today."

She didn't notice him because she was thinking about (something you dream about) _____. Troy said, "Can I carry your (household appliance) _____?" She said, "Sure, since you are acting like (name a cartoon character) _____." Troy said, "I sure wish I could just (something you want to do after school) _____."

So the two of them walked together holding (part of the body) _____. It wasn't long before they came to school, and they said, (what you say when you are surprised) "_____!" "Well, I have to say goodbye now," said Troy. "My (a musical instrument) _____ teacher is expecting me to be early so I can (something you do with friends) _____."

She said, "Oh, Troy, don't (something you say to someone you're angry with) _____ because I think you are a (describe a pet animal) _____."

Troy said, "I will always remember this day because you are so (word used to describe a food) _____."

Warm-Up: Set Up the Lesson

Gather the group together and announce the theme and the goals. Have a student read the story created in the Presession.

Focus: Openers and Roadblocks

Make copies of the reproducible flash cards and cut them apart. Say to the class, **When someone wants to talk to you, you can respond with an opener that says you want to listen or with a roadblock that stops the conversation. I will mix the cards. Then we will take turns to draw a card and read it. The rest of you will vote with traffic-police hand gestures. If the sentence is an opener to conversation, motion traffic to come. If the** sentence is a roadblock to communication, motion for traffic to stop.

Flash Cards for Openers
(Listed below are the "opener" statements.)

Tell me more about it.
Sounds like you have thought about this a long time.
Keep talking; I'm listening.
You have a lot of feelings about this, don't you?
What else are you thinking?
How do you feel about that?
What do you think about that?
How do you see it?
What does that look like to you?
What have you considered?
I hear you.
Sounds like there might be more.
That is interesting to me.

Flash Cards for Roadblocks
(Listed below are the roadblock statements.)

You don't mean that.
You shouldn't be thinking that way.
That would be the right thing to do.
You are wonderful.
I wish you would not do that.
That would be a mistake.
Let me tell you what I think.
You better not do that.
If you knew what was good for you, you would do it soon.
I can't believe you would even think that.
Don't be silly.
I'm not even going to go there.
Please reconsider that idea.
If you do that, you are in big trouble.
It sounds like you are just jealous.
That reminds me of something that happened to me.

Activity: What Would a Helper Say?

Divide into teams of four to six people. Distribute the Team Page and ask participants to complete Teamwork Part A together. Be available to respond to questions.

Bible Reflection: Team Page

Follow the directions for Teamwork Part B on the Team Page and discuss as a class.

Closing: Prayer Time

Bring the group back together in a large circle. Make sure they have their Team Page. Go around the circle, beginning and ending with you. Allow each person to read their prayer from Teamwork Part B.

Teamwork Part A

What Would a Helper Say?

Choose the best listening response from the choices below:

Speaker # 1: "I'm bored, nobody cares about me."

☐ "Well, get busy doing something worthwhile, and you won't be so bored."

☐ "Oh, I care about you, and I know lots of others who care too."

☐ "You feel bored and lonely?"

Speaker # 2: "I was so mad at her. She turned her back on me again. Just when I thought we were friends."

☐ "You are upset because you thought she was a friend."

☐ "What did you do to cause her to turn on you?"

☐ "If she is going to be like that, you don't need her friendship."

Speaker # 3: "My girlfriend keeps putting me down. I wish she would treat me better."

☐ "Yeah, my boyfriend does the same thing."

☐ "You should dump her. The sooner the better."

☐ "Sounds like you get upset when your girlfriend uses put-downs against you. Sounds like you wish it would be different."

Teamwork Part B

Bible Reflection

Read the following passage and circle all the positive actions. Cross out all the negative actions.

> By contrast, the fruit of the Spirit is love, joy, peace, patience, kindness, generosity, faithfulness, gentleness, and self-control. There is no law against such things. And those who belong to Christ Jesus have crucified the flesh with its passions and desires. If we live by the Spirit, let us also be guided by the Spirit. Let us not become conceited, competing against one another, envying one another. My friends, if anyone is detected in a transgression, you who have received the Spirit should restore such a one in a spirit of gentleness. Take care that you yourselves are not tempted. Bear one another's burdens, and in this way you will fulfill the law of Christ. (Galatians 5:22–6:2 NRSV)

Living by the Spirit includes listening to each other as we bear one another's burdens.

Whose work is it to stop sin and bear the fruit of the Spirit? (Of course, the Holy Spirit's work.) How has Christ encouraged us and listened to us? How does it feel that you are given the Holy Spirit, who enables you to bear this fruit?

Complete the following prayer stem and be prepared to pray it in the large group.

Oh, Holy Spirit, help me to
_____, and thank
You, Jesus, for Your love and
_____
_____.

Flash Cards for Openers

Tell me more about it.

You have a lot of feelings about this, don't you?

Sounds like you have thought about this a long time.

Keep talking; I'm listening.

What do you think about that?

What else are you thinking?

How do you feel about that?

What have you considered?

How do you see it?

What does that look like to you?

That is interesting to me.

I hear you.

Sounds like there might be more.

Flash Cards for Roadblocks

That reminds me of something that happened to me.

You don't mean that.

You shouldn't be thinking that way.

That would be the right thing to do.

You are wonderful.

I wish you would not do that.

That would be a mistake.

Let me tell you what I think.

You better not do that.

If you knew what was good for you, you would do it soon.

I can't believe you would even think that.

Don't be silly.

I'm not even going to go there.

Please reconsider that idea.

If you do that, you are in big trouble.

It sounds like you are just jealous.

18B   **Team Page** *Flash Cards*

Stop the Flow!
Discovering Communication Roadblocks

19

Introduction

Some phrases and words discourage or even halt good communication. This lesson will encourage caring friends to avoid roadblocks.

Key Concept

Communication roadblocks include easy solutions, put-downs, and smoke screens.

Goals

Youth will identify replies that block good communication.

Bible Reference

Jesus heals the man who had been born blind (John 9:1–37).

Presession: Building Roadblocks

Put out play dough and encourage the youth to make sculptures of different kinds of barriers: stop signs, traffic barricades, roadblocks, retaining walls, dikes, and so on. Have them describe their creation. If time allows, have them talk about one barrier between God and them.

Lesson Overview

Activity	Summary	Goal	Materials	Time
Presession	Sculpture	Build relationships while working on an art project	Play dough	Before class time
Warm-up	Four-Corner Continuum	Mix up the youth and introduce the communication theme	Four Signs: Always, Sometimes, Seldom, and Never	10 minutes
Focus	Teach roadblocks to communication	Youth see the three basic communication roadblocks	Teachers Guide, newsprint or chalkboard	15 minutes
Activity	Team challenge	Identify more roadblocks	Team Page, cardboard for three signs for every five youth, marking pens	15 minutes
Bible Reflection	John 9:1–37	Youth see how the Pharisees blocked communication	Team Page, pencils	15 minutes
Closing	Singing	Blind Man	Songbook, recorded music (optional)	5 minutes

Warm-Up: Go to the Corner

Use the four corners of the room to help youth think about communication. Put one of these large signs in each corner of the room: Always, Sometimes, Seldom, Never. Say, **When I read each statement, respond by going to the corner that reflects your reaction. When you get there, discuss your reaction with the people in that corner. Now respond to the following:**

1. My parents really listen to me.
2. My teachers really listen to me.
3. My friends really listen to me.
4. People in general are good listeners.
5. I feel listened to …

Focus: Three Stoppers

Say, Today we will take a closer look at what makes communication ineffective. Some communication habits actually stop conversations. **What are some things you have seen or experienced that would make you discontinue a conversation with someone?** List these on newsprint or chalkboard. Add the following if the youth haven't thought of them:

- Criticizing what was said.
- Correcting unimportant facts.
- Embarrassing someone around others.
- Teasing the speaker (may cause distrust).
- Giving commands or orders with little input or choice.
- Warning of the consequences of behavior.
- Offering unsolicited advice instead of letting them solve things.
- Judging someone as right or wrong.
- Arguing over views (even when playing the devil's advocate).
- Advocating only one point of view instead of different opinions.
- Changing the subject to a more interesting topic.
- Analyzing a person and sharing conclusions.
- Giving insincere (manipulative) praises.
- Giving insincere (manipulative) sympathy.

Activity: Team Challenge

Hand out the Team Page. Divide the youth into groups of five or six. Distribute cardboard and have them make the roadblock signs as instructed in Teamwork Part A. Choose two volunteers to read each set of statements. After listening carefully, each team will determine which of the roadblocks has been used and hold up the appropriate roadblock sign: Smoke Screens, Put-Downs, Easy Solutions. Teams that correctly identify the roadblock are awarded points. The team receiving the greatest number of points wins.

Bible Reflection: Team Page

Have youth complete Teamwork Part B on the Team Page.

Closing: Music

Sing "Blind Man Stood by the Road and He Cried."

Other Resources

Lost and Found's album with the song "Blind Man." See order information in the appendix.

#1—Statement: My parents won't let me go to the party. They say I'll get into trouble.

#2—Response: What did you do to make them not trust you?

#1—Statement: That group of kids are such snobs they would never ask me to go. I hate them.

#2—Response: Just get as far away from them as you can.

#1—Statement: I just got my report card … my grades stink. My parents are going to kill me! I'll be grounded for the rest of my life!!

#2—Response: Don't worry. This won't be the worst thing to come along.

#1—Statement: I worked hard on this speech, but I just know I'll mess up in front of everybody when I have to give it. It is so embarrassing.

#2—Response: Why don't you pretend you are sick that day?

#1—Statement: My sister can't keep her mouth shut! She always tells everyone about stuff like this!

#2—Response: So, who cares if everyone knows? Hey, did you hear about Jodie?

#1—Statement: I really hate math. I used to be good at it, but now I'm lost.

#2—Response: Well, it looks like you're not going to be a brain surgeon after all!

#1—Statement: My parents argue so much. I wouldn't be surprised if they split up.

#2—Response: Just live with the one who can get you the most stuff!

#1—Statement: I just found out I have to get my tonsils out. I hate hospitals! I hate needles! Doctors give me the creeps!

#2—Response: Oh, come on! Kids get tonsils out all the time. It's easy, and you get to eat lots of cool stuff.

#1—Statement: I'm so ugly. No one will ask me to the dance.

#2—Response: You know, when you're so negative, I don't feel like hanging around you either!

#1—Statement: I really hate my English teacher. He says I won't pass his class. Where do they get teachers like that?

#2—Response: I did okay in his class. Aren't you doing your homework?

Three Roadblocks

Easy Solutions
I know what is best for you.

Put-Downs
I am smarter than you are.

Smoke Screens
Forget about it.

Teamwork Part A

Roadblocks: Put-downs, smoke screens, easy solutions

Make an 8″ × 11″ sign for each of these different road-blocks. Listen to each statement and response. Have the group decide which sign to hold up.

Teamwork Part B

Bible Reflection

Read the story of the blind man. Identify the roadblocks illustrated in the underlined passages.

As he walked along, he saw a man blind from birth. His disciples asked him, "Rabbi, who sinned, this man or his parents, that he was born blind?" Jesus answered, "Neither this man nor his parents sinned; he was born blind so that God's works might be revealed in him. We must work the works of him who sent me while it is day; night is coming when no one can work. As long as I am in the world, I am the light of the world." When he had said this, he spat on the ground and made mud with the saliva and spread the mud on the man's eyes, saying to him, "Go, wash in the pool of Siloam" (which means Sent). Then he went and washed and came back able to see. …

So they said again to the blind man, "What do you say about him? It was your eyes he opened." He said, "He is a prophet." <u>The Jews did not believe that he had been blind and had received his sight until they called the parents of the man who had received his sight</u> and asked them, "Is this your son, who you say was born blind? How then does he now see?" His parents answered, "We know that this is our son, and that he was born blind; but we do not know how it is that now he sees, nor do we know who opened his eyes. Ask him; he is of age. He will speak for him-self." His parents said this because they were afraid of the Jews; for the Jews had already agreed that anyone who confessed Jesus to be the Messiah would be put out of the syna-

Scripture: © NRSV.   © 1999 CPH

gogue. Therefore his parents said, "He is of age; ask him." So for the second time they called the man who had been blind, and they said to him, "Give glory to God! We know that this man is a sinner." He answered, "I do not know whether he is a sinner. One thing I do know, that though I was blind, now I see." They said to him, "What did he do to you? How did he open your eyes?" He answered them, "I have told you already, and you would not listen. Why do you want to hear it again? Do you also want to become his disciples?" Then they reviled him, saying, "You are his disciple, but we are disciples of Moses. We know that God has spoken to Moses, but as for this man, we do not know where he comes from."

The man answered, "Here is an astonishing thing! You do not know where he comes from, and yet he opened my eyes. We know that God does not listen to sinners, but he does listen to one who worships him and obeys his will. Never since the world began has it been heard that anyone opened the eyes of a person born blind. If this man were not from God, he could do nothing." They answered him, "You were born entirely in sins, and are you trying to teach us?" And they drove him out. Jesus heard that they had driven him out, and when he found him, he said, "Do you believe in the Son of Man?" He answered, "And who is he, sir? Tell me, so that I may believe in him." Jesus said to him, "You have seen him, and the one speaking with you is he." (John 9:1–7,17–37 NRSV)

How does Jesus handle the opposition?

How does the Gospel of Jesus Christ, coming through Baptism and the Word of God, overcome roadblocks? When does God's love and forgiveness overpower our objections? What does it mean for us?

Team Page *Stop the Flow!* 19C

20 What Is Your Name?
Name-Calling and Respecting Identity

Introduction

Communication skills are improved when youth describe what they see and hear firsthand, rather than sharing what they think or feel about someone. For instance, it may be better to tell your school-locker partner, "That messy science project you put on top of my jacket makes my jacket stink," than to say, "You inconsiderate slob!" The first is factual information; the second is a verbal put-down based on your reactive feelings. It is a judgment that causes defensiveness or shame.

Key Concept

Names are important. God loves us enough to tell us His name. He gave His Son the name Jesus because Jesus is our Savior. There is power in a name. A good name is to be protected; hurtful name-calling is destructive and should be avoided.

Goals

Participants will reflect upon their name and how knowing and using someone's name with respect is a skill for peer counseling. They will discover some of the names for Jesus and discuss how to build self-esteem through better communication.

Bible Reference

Isaiah 9:6–7 and Philippians 2:5–10

Lesson Overview

Activity	Summary	Goal	Materials	Time
Presession	CrossName puzzle	See how names are connected with Jesus	Mural paper or newsprint, marking pens	Arrival time
Warm-up	Guess the Bible character	Name recognition of Bible characters	Name tags and marking pens, Bibles	15 minutes
Focus	Name, don't blame	Describe behaviors rather than people	Chalkboard or newsprint (for quotation), Bible	10 minutes
Activity	Practice alternatives to name-calling	Identify a behavior without a put-down	Team Page, paper, pencils	20 minutes
Bible Reflection	Isaiah 9:6–7	Names for Jesus	Team Page, pencils	5 minutes
Closing	Acrostic	Around the circle of friends	Team Page	10 minutes

Presession: CrossName Puzzle

Cover about a six feet by three feet area of wall with mural paper or newsprint. Title the paper "CrossName Puzzle." Write "Jesus" and "Christ" as shown below in big letters in the middle of the paper. As the participants arrive, invite them to use a marking pen and write their name, sharing a letter from the pattern or another student's name.

```
          J
          E
  C H R I S T
          U
          S
```

Warm-Up: The Name Game

Announce that you are going to play a Bible-name game. Before class, use the following list to make a different biblical name tag for each student, which is affixed to their back. The goal is for each student to guess the name of the biblical person on their back. The only way to find out is to ask other people yes/no questions. The only answers allowed are "yes," "no," or "I don't know." Move around the room until everyone has guessed the name on their back or three to five minutes have elapsed. Ask youth to return to their table and help each other to learn about the names they have been given. Turn to the Bible passage to find out more about their character.

Adam, Genesis 2:19
Eve, Genesis 3:20
Methuselah, Genesis 5:27
Noah, Genesis 7:6
Abraham, Genesis 17:3–5
Sarah, Genesis 17:3–5
Isaac, Genesis 17:19
Rebekah, Genesis 25:19–27
Esau, Genesis 25:19–27
Jacob, Genesis 28:10–13
Rachel, Genesis 29:16–20
Joseph (Old Testament), Genesis 37:3
Moses, Exodus 2:5–10
Miriam, Exodus 15:19–21
Joshua, Joshua 6:13 and 24:15
Samson, Judges 16:6–9
Delilah, Judges 16:6–9
Ruth, Ruth 1:15–19
Samuel, 1 Samuel 2:26–28
David, 1 Samuel 17:48–51
Solomon, 1 Kings 4:29–30
Elijah, 2 Kings 2:8–12
Daniel, Daniel 6:16–22
Jonah, Jonah 1:15–17

Job, Job 1:7–12
Esther, Esther 2:15–16 and 7:1–7
Isaiah, Isaiah 1:1
Matthew, Matthew 9:9
John the Baptist, Matthew 3:1–3
Peter, Matthew 14:26–30
Paul, Acts 9:3–8
Zacchaeus, Luke 19:1–5
Elizabeth, Luke 1:13
Mary, Luke 2:30–35
Timothy, Acts 16:1–3
Nicodemus, John 3:1–4
Barnabas, Acts 12:25–13:3

In the large group, discuss how it might (does) feel to be named after one of these biblical characters.

Focus: Name It

Make the following points to the entire group:

- Names are important. It is difficult to have relationships with people until you learn their name.
- When God told Moses His name, it became the beginning of a relationship with him and the children of Israel.
- The many names for Jesus help us better understand who He is.
- Bad names are powerful and hurtful.

Ask a volunteer to read this passage to the group:

Your attitude should be the same as that of Christ Jesus: Who, being in very nature God, did not consider equality with God something to be grasped, but made Himself nothing, taking the very nature of a servant, being made in human likeness. And being found in appearance as a man, He humbled Himself and became obedient to death—even death on a cross! Therefore God exalted Him to the highest place and gave Him the name that is above every name, that at the name of Jesus every knee should bow, in heaven and on earth and under the earth. (Philippians 2:5–10 NIV)

Write this statement on newsprint or a chalkboard: "Sticks and stones may break my bones but words will never hurt me." Ask, **What does this statement mean to you? Is it true? How can name-calling hurt just as badly as sticks and stones?**

The name of Jesus is wonderful to our ears because of who He is and what He did. How do you feel when you hear His name? How does it feel that we are baptized "in the name of the Father and of the Son and of the Holy Spirit"? How does being called by His name (Christian) make you feel about yourself, regardless of your name? How does your name sound to you? If it sounds wonderful to you, it may be because you have been given love, affirmation, and forgiveness. If you don't like the sound of your name, why is that? Sometimes it is because a person has been given lots of criticism, condemnation, or ridicule.

When a behavior is unacceptable, you should not ignore it. It should be dealt with. When you confront someone who calls others hurtful names, it may help if you show love and care for them, which may protect their self-esteem. The best way is not to call them a name back, but to simply reflect on what you hear them say in simple, basic, accurate terms.

Activity: Team Page

Form teams of four to six and distribute the Team Page, paper, and pencils. Go over the instructions for Teamwork Parts A and B and tell students to complete them in the given time. Walk among them and encourage them to stay on task. Help them if they need clarification.

Bible Reflection: Team Page

Have one or more students read the passage aloud from Teamwork Part C on the Team Page. Have students underline Jesus' names. Discuss the questions on the sheet. If time allows, have each student make a name tag of their name of Jesus that they find most assuring. Have them explain how God's name becomes part of who each person is.

Closing: Team Page

Bring the group together in a circle. Have each youth read the acrostic of their names. Close with the prayer on the Team Page.

> Dear God, thank You for our names. We are glad that You let us know Your name. Because one of Your names is Savior, our names are connected to each other forever. In Jesus' name we give thanks and pray. Amen.

Teamwork Part A

Write your name vertically along the left column of a sheet of paper and write a word that describes you with each of the letters of your name (see example for Fred).

Fun
Real
Excellent
Delightful

Teamwork Part B

In the Name of Love

People can be hurt by the things others **do** as well as by what they **say**. This exercise will let you practice what to say when someone does a hurtful or unacceptable thing. Suggest responses for each of these categories.

What They Do	What Not to Say	A Better Way
Speaking loudly	You are a loudmouth.	You are talking so loud it is uncomfortable for me.
Loudly slurping with their straw	Don't be a slob.	You are slurping loud enough to be heard over our talking.

Teamwork Part C

The prophet Isaiah foretells the birth of the Messiah, including many names by which He will be known or described. Underline those names.

Which of these names is most meaningful to you? Why? Which name gives you the most assurance that God loves and cares for you for eternity?

> For a child has been born for us, a son given to us; authority rests upon his shoulders; and he is named Wonderful Counselor, Mighty God, Everlasting Father, Prince of Peace. His authority shall grow continually, and there shall be endless peace for the throne of David and his kingdom. He will establish and uphold it with justice and with righteousness from this time onward and forevermore. The zeal of the LORD of hosts will do this. (Isaiah 9:6–7 NRSV)

21 Who Owns the Problem?
Identify Problem Ownership

Introduction

One important communication skill is the ability to identify who "owns" a problem. Dr. David Elkind points out that a young adolescent's view of the world is shaped by a false audience. He describes a form of narcissism in which youth assume that everyone sees the world exactly as they do, where they play the central role. In this lesson, youth will learn skills to help them identify whether the problem is truly theirs or someone else's. Youth will then be better able to identify possible approaches to improve a relationship where there is conflict. This lesson will make use of the techniques of staying objective, using assertiveness skills, and applying positive listening skills.

Key Concept

It is an important relationship skill to identify a problem source and how to best approach it. "My problem" is best addressed by effective use of assertiveness skills. "Your problem" is best addressed when the owner of the problem feels listened to and cared about. "Our problem" means that there is a shared problem requiring courage, patience, good listening skills, assertiveness, and time to brainstorm possible solutions.

Goals

Participants will explore the concept of problem ownership.

Lesson Overview

Activity	Summary	Goal	Materials	Time
Presession	Yap, Yap, Yap	Evaluate problem ownership	Prerecorded segments of afternoon talk shows, VCR, TV	5–10 minutes before class begins
Warm-up	"Pass the Button" game	Youth will identify "it"'s problem	Chairs, button	15 minutes
Focus	Three-part deal	Youth will recognize three different ownership categories	Team Page, printed instructions	15 minutes
Activity	Make a Stand	Youth will identify the three ownership areas	Three signs designating "My Problem," "Your Problem," and "Our Problem"; situations listed in the instructions	10 minutes
Bible Reflection	Luke 6:35–48	Apply God's wisdom	Team Page with Bible reference	5 minutes
Closing	Group paragraph	Review of problem-identification	Newsprint, markers	5 minutes

Bible Reference

Luke 6:35–48 NRSV

Presession

Students can role-play an afternoon talk show with a designated topic that involves problem ownership, complete with guest speaker and audience. (If permission is granted, the instructor might videotape a real afternoon talk show that exemplifies the issue.) The subject matter should be chosen carefully. Ask youth to identify the problem and determine which of the characters "owns" the problem. Help them identify which individuals are trying to transfer their problem to someone else. Discuss why some people might avoid owning up to a problem, and talk about how to make sure all of the involved parties can be brought into the conversation.

Warm-Up

Play "Pass the Button." Youth sit on chairs arranged in a circle. Someone is designated as "it." The person who is "it" stands in the center of the circle as the youth pass a button or another small item around the circle. The goal is to keep the button going without "it" guessing who is passing it. Fake passes are acceptable to throw "it" off base. The button must be kept moving at all times. When "it" guesses which youth actually is holding the button, that person then must become the "it."

Focus: Three-Part Deal

Say, **When you encounter a problem, one key ingredient in solving it is to determine exactly whose problem it is. There are basically three ways to view situations: as my problem, your problem, or our problem. Knowing which it is will help you determine how to solve it. When it is "my problem," no one else is directly affected. I am the only one who finds the situation unacceptable. Others may be affected eventually because it angers me, but the problem itself is not the issue with them. When I see the problem as mine, I know I need to assertively express my needs and concerns to others without casting blame.** Use the cartoon on the Team Page and have the youth list examples of things that might be considered "my problem." Then say, **The next illustration on your Team Page refers to situations that are considered "your problem." That means someone else is affect-**ed by a situation that doesn't necessarily bother you at all. Sometimes you are the cause; sometimes it is something totally unrelated to you. Many times when we care about others we "join" them and make the problem worse by losing our own objectivity. In our effort to help, we commiserate with them, or worse yet, we add their problem to our shoulders without taking it from theirs. The better solution is to put your listening skills to work. Many times friends just need someone to listen to them. The best thing you can do is listen for feelings. If you are the cause for their concern, listening for feelings and showing understanding is especially important. There may be serious situations in which you might suggest they also talk to an adult they trust.** Use the Team Page to list topics that could be considered "your problem."

Then say, **The third category is "our problem," where the relationship is at risk. You may both be angry and hurt. It takes both of you to make things right, but it may be up to you to initiate the solution, using good listening and assertiveness skills. When you have listened for understanding, both of you can brainstorm solutions to the problem. Both of you win when the relationship is restored.** Have the youth list situations that could be considered "our problem." Try to relate realistic examples.

Activity: Make a Stand

Designate and label three areas of the room as either "My Problem," "Your Problem," or "Our Problem" areas. Have youth listen to the situations listed below and physically move to the area that they believe best represents ownership of the problem. Be ready for disagreements. Discuss why they made their choices.

Situation A: John is a friend who is rather short for a seventh grader. Last year he tried out for the basketball team and almost got cut. He hasn't improved very much since last season, and when he tried out this year, he didn't make it. He's really upset and asks if he can come over to your house.

Situation B: You have a crush on the same person that your good friend does. Both of you have been flirting with this person, but lately when you have been around this person, your friend gets real quiet and won't talk to you for a while afterwards.

Situation C: You are sitting at lunch with your family and your little brother accidentally splashes his ketchup on your pants. Your brother feels terrible.

Situation D: You have been hanging out with the same two people all year. The three of you have had a lot of fun together. But lately one of the friends has not invited you along on things.

Situation E: Nicole, a friend, is crying in the hallway at school. When you ask her what is wrong, she explains that Mrs. Brown, her English teacher, has accused her of cheating. Nicole will not pass the class if she fails this test.

Situation F: Jean, your best friend, always copies your math homework. When you tire of furnishing her with the answers and tell her "no," she stops speaking to you. You miss her friendship.

Bible Reflection: Team Page

Read the Bible verse written on the Team Page. Discuss applications to today's lesson.

Closing: Group Paragraph

Divide the youth into groups of four by counting off numerically. One group member should be designated as the recorder. Each group is to list as many ways as possible that this lesson could be helpful (take two minutes). The group with the longest list wins.

Notes for understanding who owns the problem:

My Problem   Your Problem   Our Problem

_____   _____   _____

_____   _____   _____

_____   _____   _____

_____   _____   _____

_____   _____   _____

Teamwork

Read the following Bible passage. How does it apply to what we have been talking about today? Whose problem was our sin?

How does Jesus' love for us—dying on the cross for our sin—motivate our love for others?

But love your enemies, do good, and lend, expecting nothing in return. Your reward will be great, and you will be children of the Most High; for he is kind to the ungrateful and the wicked. Be merciful, just as your Father is merciful. "Do not judge, and you will not be judged; do not condemn, and you will not be condemned. Forgive, and you will be forgiven; give, and it will be given to you. A good measure, pressed down, shaken together, running over, will be put into your lap; for the measure you give will be the measure you get back." (Luke 6:35–48 NRSV)

22 Talk to My Hand
Conflict Management

Introduction

Conflicts are a common part of life. The purpose of this lesson is to introduce/reinforce positive techniques for handling conflictive situations. There are two common ways that disagreement may be communicated. A controller offers no choice to others, but uses techniques like ordering, threatening, punishing, and even conditional or manipulative praise. An influencer shares, makes suggestions, advises, and teaches. Influencers try to give others choices to help them feel like part of the team process.

Key Concept

Youth will recognize conflict management styles and identify whether they themselves are controllers or influencers.

Goals

Youth will learn to identify controller and influencer techniques.

Bible Reference

Genesis 25 (NRSV)

Lesson Overview

Activity	Summary	Goal	Materials	Time
Presession	Find your match	Mix the group and introduce the lesson	Index cards with names of antagonists/protagonists	Arrival/Presession
Warm-up	You Win	Game to warm up the group and introduce feelings of inclusion and exclusion	None	10 to 15 minutes
Focus	Controller and Influencer	Help youth identify the difference in conflict management styles	Newsprint, marker	5 minutes
Activity	Role-play activity to highlight differences	Clarify distinction in conflict management styles	Team Page, video camera (optional)	20 minutes
Bible Reflection	Evaluate styles of Esau and Jacob	Learn from biblical conflict how to avoid trigger phrases	Bible or Teachers Guide	5 minutes
Closing	Team songs	Youth write songs that the group sings	Team Page	15 minutes

Presession: Find Your Match

Before class, prepare a pair of index cards for every two students, with the name of a protagonist on one card and the name of a matching antagonist on the other. Distribute one card to each student. Their task is to find the match to their card by asking only yes-or-no questions. Suggested pairs: Batman and the Joker, Peter Pan and Captain Hook, Popeye and Brutus, Bart Simpson and Principal Skinner, Tom and Jerry, Robin Hood and the Sheriff of Nottingham. Make up others.

Warm-Up: You Win

Have students stand, and instruct them to form groups of as many people as the number you call out. When the number is called, students are to join hands and make a group of that size. People who do not join the group are eliminated from the rest of the game. Start with the number that is one less than the total number of students. One person will be left out and must sit down. Continue until only two people are left.

Focus: Name It

Say, **When a conflict happens between two people, many times the way someone handles it determines the outcome. Conflict that is managed properly can sometimes lead to closer relationships than if conflict is avoided altogether. Two of the most basic approaches to conflict are control and influence. A controller tries to get his/her own way by bullying or bossing. Threats are often heard, sometimes accompanied by punishment. A controller may also use praise to manipulate feelings or actions in someone else. The bottom line is that the controller does not give another person any choice. It's the controller's way or nothing.**

An influencer, on the other hand, does not use power to control another person. Influencers give suggestions when appropriate and share their own personal experience. If another way to approach something might be helpful, they teach the other person how to do it. An individual who influences others gives them options and choices.

Involve the youth in a discussion of examples of both controllers and influencers. Create these two headings on newsprint and list examples under each.

Activity: Team Page

Distribute the Team Page and divide into groups of four to six youth. In Teamwork Part A, have the youth list five to seven different conflict situations. Each group chooses one situation to role-play using both styles to "address" the problem. If possible, videotape the role play and play it back, noticing the effects of each style.

Bible Reflection: Wait for the Word

Divide youth into groups. Assign one of the names of the Bible story characters and the appropriate dialogue to each group. Whenever the name of their character is read as the story is told, have that group say this response.
Lord—"Alleluia!"
Rebekah—"Praise God!"
Isaac—"Oh yeah!"
Esau—"Whoa!"
Jacob—"Gotcha!"

> Isaac was forty years old when he married Rebekah. … Isaac prayed to the LORD for his wife, because she was barren; and the LORD granted his prayer, and his wife Rebekah conceived. The children struggled together within her; and she said, "If it is to be this way, why do I live?" So she went to inquire of the LORD. And the LORD said to her, "Two nations are in your womb, and two peoples born of you shall be divided; the one shall be stronger than the other, the elder shall serve the younger." When her time to give birth was at hand, there were twins in her womb. The first came out red, all his body like a hairy mantle; so they named him Esau. Afterward his brother came out, with his hand gripping Esau's heel; so he was named Jacob. Isaac was sixty years old when she bore them. When the boys grew up, Esau was a skillful hunter, a man of the field, while Jacob was a quiet man, living in tents. Isaac loved Esau, because he was fond of game; but Rebekah loved Jacob. Once when Jacob was cooking a stew, Esau came in from the field, and he was famished.

Esau said to Jacob, "Let me eat some of that red stuff, for I am famished!" (Therefore he was called Edom.) Jacob said, "First sell me your birthright." Esau said, "I am about to die; of what use is a birthright to me?" Jacob said, "Swear to me first." So he swore to him, and sold his birthright to Jacob. Then Jacob gave Esau bread and lentil stew, and he ate and drank, and rose and went his way. Thus Esau despised his birthright. (Genesis 25:20–34 NRSV)

Have the youth suggest the possible conflicts between Jacob, Esau, Rebekah, and Isaac. Discuss the ways conflict was handled in the story. Where was God in the midst of the conflict? How did He use conflict to make His will unfold in the lives of this family? How did God use conflict to bring about the greatest event for our salvation when Jesus died on the cross? Who benefits from that conflict?

Closing: Sing It

Use Teamwork Part B for a closing.

Teamwork Part A

List the most common things that cause conflict for youth.

1)

2)

3)

4)

5)

6)

7)

Take Note!

Conflicts happen. Two different response styles are explored in today's session: influencer(s) and controller(s). List the characteristics of each one.

Controller(s) ...

Influencer(s) ...

Parts for Bible Response

Lord—"Alleluia!"

Rebekah—"Praise God!"

Isaac—"Oh yeah!"

Esau—"Whoa!"

Jacob—"Gotcha!"

Teamwork Part B

Each team is to write song lyrics based on a popular country-and-western melody. Make the first verse describe a controller and the second verse describe an influencer. Remember, a true country song contains the theme of a train, your mother, a broken heart, or your faithful dog. Tunes to consider: "Rocky Top," "Achy Breaky Heart," "I'm Leaving Here a Better Man."

23 The 4 Cs

Recognizing Coping Styles

Introduction

How do you respond when you are under pressure to conform? What do you do in a conflict situation? Caring friends learn to assert themselves with honesty and are ready to listen. This lesson will introduce the concept and hold up a model for Christian response.

Key Concept

Those whom Jesus has called to be His friends are given the strength to face difficulty and conflict with the assurance of His everlasting, perfect peace.

Goals

The focus of this session is to help participants distinguish between four response styles when in pressure situations. The youth will be able to identify their own responses and discuss responses with others.

Bible Reference

Peter at the arrest of Jesus (Mark 14)

Presession: Loud-Mouth Lucy

Make transparencies of cartoon characters that are demonstrating anger (i.e., Dagwood from "Blondie," Lucy from "Peanuts," and Sarge from "Beetle Bailey"). Project one on a screen where youth can see it as they arrive. Let the youth write several different balloons of what the character might be saying. If another transparency sheet is needed, have one ready.

Lesson Overview

Activity	Summary	Goal	Materials	Time
Presession	Cartoon characters	Introduce the theme by demonstrating emotions	Overhead projector, transparency, cartoon figures, overhead marking pens	Presession/ arrival until class time
Warm-up	Game of Smiles	Youth attempt to control their emotions	None	15 minutes
Focus	Teach the four coping styles	Youth identify the four styles from written choices	Chalkboard or newsprint, Team Page	15 minutes
Activity	"Take a Stand" role play	Youth act out honesty with listening responses	Team Page	15 minutes
Bible Reflection	Mark 14—Jesus arrested in the garden	See the various styles with Jesus in control	Team Page	15 minutes
Closing	Prayer		Teachers Guide	2 minutes

Warm-Up: Smile Honey!

Ask the group to be seated in a circle. Choose a youth to be the first "it." This person may go to anyone in the circle and attempt to make them smile. The person does this with their facial expressions and by using only these words: "Honey, if you love me, won't you please smile for me?" The person must say back (without smiling or laughing), "Honey, I love you, but I just can't smile." If unsuccessful, "it" moves on to someone else until someone smiles when responding. Then they exchange places.

Focus: Coping Styles

Distribute the Team Page and have students check off a typical response to the examples given in Teamwork Part A. Go over each response with the youth and categorize each statement into one of the four different coping styles.

Say, **People respond differently when under pressure. Imagine that you and your friends want to go to two different places. This can create pressure and conflict. Others may want to go putt-putt golfing, but you hate putt-putt golf. You'd rather go bowling. How do you respond to your friends when they make their suggestion? Why?** Allow students to list various factors that would influence their decision. Then say, **Look at the statements on the Team Page. Choose the way you might normally respond to the person making the statement.**

After they have had time to respond, introduce the four common types of responses to pressure situations. **People respond to things differently. One type of response is to fight, often using put-downs, sarcasm, or snippy, argumentative responses, or even by no longer counting someone as a friend.** Write "Fight" on the chalkboard or newsprint and invite them to share examples where this response was used.

Another typical response is to escape. (Write the word.) **Instead of honestly sharing their desires or feelings, they may make excuses ("I think I hear my mother calling me") and avoid the situation. Escape doesn't always mean you physically leave. Sometimes you can put people off by words or phrases like "in a minute" or "hold on." Of course, the hope is that they will forget and you never will have to deal with it.**

A third response to a pressure situation is to submit. (Write the word.) **You may be afraid to share your needs or desires because of the fear that it might cost you the friendship. So you do whatever they want you to do and never stand up for what you want to do. The** risk is that you become pretty unhappy or they see you as rather boring. They will never know how you really feel and therefore never really get to know you.

The fourth way to respond to a pressure situation is to be honest (write the word) **and share what your needs are. Responding honestly will give others the opportunity to know you and perhaps come to a mutually agreeable solution. Remember, an "I statement" followed by listening can be very helpful. You are a worthy person. Let others know how you feel.**

Discuss the positive and negative effects of the answers in Teamwork Part A. Identify which responses typify fight, escape, submission, and honesty.

Activity: "Take a Stand" Role Play

Pairs of youth are to take turns practicing assertive and honest responses to situations. Assign one youth to be (A) and the other (B). They should enact role play 1 from Teamwork Part B. Then they switch roles for role play 2.

After they have had some time to practice, ask, **What do you think would happen next?**
- **How would the relationship be affected?**
- **How might the speaker feel after hearing that response?**
- **How do you feel when trying to be assertive and then listening?**

Bible Reflection

Read Mark 14:42–50. Have the youth complete Teamwork Part C on the Team Page and discuss the different styles of the characters. They could work in teams or alone and then discuss their answers in the whole group. Ask, **How important is it to be honest? Why? What if God hadn't been honest about our sin? How is the message of Jesus' death and resurrection an honest message of God's love? What has God's honesty done to our relationship? How does your honesty with God improve the relationship?**

Closing

Close with this prayer:

Dear Jesus, You have so much love for people that You were kind and forgiving to Your enemies. In Your kindness You were strong, and we praise You for Your gentle majesty. Send the Holy Spirit so that we can be more like You and stand for what we believe with peace and love. Help us to always rejoice in Your honest message of love for us. In Jesus' name. Amen.

Teamwork Part A

Choose a response you might make to the following statements.

1. You are busy with a project and your older sister says, "Go get my brush from the car."

Your response:

a. Get it yourself!

b. I'll get it later.

c. I can't. I'm in the middle of a project.

d. Okay! (you drop everything and do it)

2. A group of friends is trying to decide what to do on Saturday afternoon. A number of suggestions have been made, but one member of the group insists on going bowling. You hate bowling! He says, "Come on! Let's quit talking about it and just go bowling."

Your response:

a. Oh, all right. But next time …

b. So who died and made you sheriff?

c. I can't. I just remembered my mother needs me to babysit for my neighbor.

d. I really don't enjoy bowling. Let's think of something we all like to do.

3. You are at a friend's house and you both want to play his newest computer game. He insists on starting first and won't give you a chance to play. You are getting impatient. He says, "Just cool it. You will get your turn. It's my game!"

Your response:

a. You don't say anything and continue to wait.

b. I can't believe you're being such a jerk!

c. It's time for me to go home.

d. I'm getting tired of waiting. I'm going to find something else to do.

4. You and a friend were dropped off at a store to shop. You thought that your friend's parents were to pick you up at a designated time. You have to be home by a certain time and must leave now to make it. Your friend spots someone and doesn't want to leave. Your friend says, "We're not going now. Didn't you see who just came in? Besides, I have to call first."

Your response:

a. Well, whatever the princess (prince) wants …

b. I've got to get home. I promised my parents.

c. I guess my parents won't be too upset.

d. I'll call my sister to come get me.

23A

Teamwork Part B

To do this role play you need to be in pairs. Choose one youth to be (A) and the other (B).

Role Play One

(A) You want B to call a person of the opposite sex and find out if they like you. You are dying to go out with this person, but you can't get up enough nerve to talk to them. You ask your friend to find out … but you don't want it to be too obvious.

Role Play One

(B) You listen carefully to what (A) wants, but you do not want to make the call. You tell (A) clearly and honestly without putting them down. State your reasons, and then listen carefully to their response; then restate your honest opinion and say "no."

Role Play Two

(A) You really want to see the show that just opened at the theater, but your parents have made other plans and can't take you. You are trying to convince (B) to ask his/her parents. After all, you took (B) to the show last week and it only seems fair. Besides, it looks like it will be a great movie.

Role Play Two

(B) You listen carefully to what (A) wants, but you do not want to go to the movies this weekend. You are not interested in that film, and you are saving your money for new clothes. You tell (A) clearly and honestly without putting them down. State your reasons, and then listen carefully to everything they say; then restate your honest opinion and say "no."

Teamwork Part C

Read about Jesus' arrest in the middle of the night and how different people reacted to this pressure situation. Can you identify the different styles of fight, escape, submission, and honesty?

[Jesus said,] "Get up, let us be going. See, my betrayer is at hand." Immediately, while he was still speaking, Judas, one of the twelve, arrived; and with him there was a crowd with swords and clubs, from the chief priests, the scribes, and the elders. Now the betrayer had given them a sign, saying, "The one I will kiss is the man; arrest him and lead him away under guard." So when he came, he went up to him at once and said, "Rabbi!" and kissed him. Then they laid hands on him and arrested him. But one of those who stood near [Peter] drew his sword and struck the slave of the high priest, cutting off his ear. Then Jesus said to them, "Have you come out with swords and clubs to arrest me as though I were a bandit? Day after day I was with you in the temple teaching, and you did not arrest me. But let the scriptures be fulfilled." All of them [the disciples] deserted him and fled. (Mark 14:42–50 NRSV)

Who	What Coping Style
Judas	_____
The Crowd	_____
Peter	_____
Jesus	_____
The Disciples	_____

24 Straight Up
Using "I Messages"

Introduction

A helpful way to assert yourself is to send an "I message." "I messages" let you express yourself clearly and honestly about issues or unacceptable behavior without blaming or using put-downs.

Key Concept

Youth will learn and practice a way to express themselves more honestly and assertively.

Goals

Youth will learn to better speak for themselves about their thoughts and feelings. They will formulate "I messages" and practice ways to use them. They will discover "I messages" in the Bible.

Bible Reference

The boy Jesus in the temple (Luke 2:41–43)

Lesson Overview

Activity	Summary	Goal	Materials	Time
Presession	Create sentences	Learn the three parts of "I messages"	Prepared messages on three different colors of index cards	Before class time
Warm-up	Complete a "T" puzzle	Examine some feelings	Team Page, scissors, paper, pencils	10 minutes
Focus	Teach the three-part "I message"	Acquaint youth with this assertiveness skill	Chalkboard or newsprint	5 minutes
Activity	Creating "I messages"	Practice in teams	Team Page, pencils, Teachers Guide situations, video camera (optional)	20 minutes
Bible Reflection	Find "I messages" in the Bible	Examine the account of the boy Jesus in the temple	Team Page, pencils	10 minutes
Closing	Positive "I messages"	End with a positive message that is not manipulative	Paper and pencil	5 minutes

Presession: Make a Sentence

Write the following on separate index cards of the same color:
When you sing out of tune,
When you pick your nose,
When you sleep in class,
When you blow bubbles,
When you eat spaghetti,
When you crack your knuckles,
When you get sick,
When you slam the door,
When you talk loudly,
When you wink your eyes,
When you tap your fingers,

Write the following on separate index cards of another color:
I feel romantic
I feel miserable
I feel disgusted
I feel inspired
I feel perplexed
I feel annoyed
I feel terrified
I feel weak
I feel bored
I feel alarmed
I feel afraid

Write the following on separate index cards of a third color:
because I lose time.
because it costs me money.
because I lose sleep.
because I can't concentrate.
because I have to do it over.
because I can't be on time.
because I won't be able to finish mine.
because I am unable to sing.
because I won't have time to eat.
because I will lose the game.
because I will be in trouble.

As the youth arrive, have them create a sentence using one card from each color. Post or display sentences. Or do a mixer, distributing cards randomly and clustering kids. Redistribute cards and repeat.

Warm-Up: "T" Puzzle

Distribute the Team Page 24B. Pass out scissors, paper, and pencils. Have youth cut out the shapes. Then explain, **These shapes are pieces to a puzzle. Your task is to arrange them into the shape of a T.**

As the youth work on the puzzle, chide them with statements like "You are not as smart as some kindergarten children who can

solve this rather quickly" or "You must not be trying very hard."

After the first person solves the puzzle, give them high praise and ask the others why they are not as clever. If no one figures out the solution, illustrate it on the chalkboard. Then have each person write how they felt while trying to solve the puzzle.

Puzzle Solution

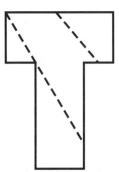

Focus: My Message about Me

Have the students review the feelings they listed after the last exercise. Have them put a "Y" by each one that talked about the teacher or someone else. Have them put an "I" by those that shared their honest feelings. For example, "The teacher is a jerk," "The teacher treats us like babies," and "This puzzle is stupid" are all "Y" (you) messages.

An "I message" describes what you think or how you feel about something. For example, "I felt frustrated trying to do this puzzle," or "When you said we were not trying hard enough, I felt embarrassed because I was trying but still couldn't solve it."

Activity: How about It?

A good "I message" usually begins with a description of the situation. "When ... happens" should describe the situation, not a judgement of someone else's role: "When I am left out of the phone circle" or "When you and your other friends are laughing while I come down the hall." Do not use words that imply your feelings about them, like "messy," "dumb," "inconsiderate," and so on. Simply describe what actually happened. Present the basic facts.

A good "I message" continues in the same sentence with a statement about the speaker's feelings. "When ... happens, I feel ..." Your feelings (remember your feelings chart from the Team Page in lesson 13?) should be honest and expressive. "I feel sad" or "I feel embarrassed" is an honest expression of how you feel. Be careful: "I feel cheated" is not a feeling, but rather is a kind of judgment about the other person.

A good "I message" then continues with an explanation of the result of the feeling. "When … happens, I feel … because …" It is best to describe any tangible effects the situation has had on you. What has this cost you in time, energy, money, or distraction? The more accurately you express the tangible effects, the more likely it is that the person will understand your side. Sometimes there is no real tangible effect; if that is so, it is still okay to send the "I message." However, the conflict may be due to a values collision, and the other person may not agree or see your side. It may boil down to differing opinions or values about something. You might still say, "When you hang out with some of the kids who do drugs, I feel uncomfortable."

Divide the group into three teams. Use the Team Page 24A, Teamwork Part A. Have students record their "I messages" on the paper you distributed during Warm-up.

As you read each situation, they will write one of the three parts of an "I message" in response. After every situation, rotate the assignments.

You might add interest and excitement—and reinforcement—to this lesson by videotaping this exercise and using it for the Warm-up in the next lesson.

Situations

1. Your friend told someone else your secret, which he had promised not to tell anyone.

2. The snack you set aside is gone because your brother (or sister) ate it.

3. Your teacher punished you for whispering, but it was the kid in the next seat who had really done it. Again.

4. You were sick and missed school and asked your neighbor to bring the assignments you missed. He forgot.

5. You are at a restaurant and the server charges you $3.00 for something you didn't order or receive. When you point this out, she says, "I'm not changing it because it's already in the computer."

6. After you spent hours on a science model, a kid on the bus asks to look at it and breaks it.

7. A friend borrows your Game Boy. When it is returned, one of the game cartridges is missing.

8. A friend has been spending a lot of time with someone who won't talk to you, even when you try.

9. You loaned $5.00 to a friend so she could sign up for the field trip. It has been two weeks and she still hasn't paid you back, even after several reminders.

10. You dropped your books in the hallway and a stranger helped you pick them up.

Bible Reflection: Team Page

Using Teamwork Part B, rewrite Mary's words to Jesus as an "I message." Then look up one or more of the suggested passages to discover some "I messages" from God to us.

Closing: Positive "I Messages"

Write a positive "I message" to someone in the room. A positive "I message" is less manipulative then a "You message."

For example, compare these two sentences: "You have all been great kids tonight." "When you listen to me and cooperate with the instructions, I feel empowered as a teacher because I am able to be heard and share my thoughts."

Share your "I message" samples aloud, or pass them as written notes.

Other Resources

Feelings Chart from Team Page, Lesson 13

Teamwork Part A

"No matter what, you're talking about yourself."

Three Part "I Message"

When you … (describe the situation in specific, non-judgmental terms).

I feel … (share the feelings that result from the situation).

Because … (describe the tangible effect their behavior has on you).

Assertive "I message":
"When you use my pencil and don't give it back, I feel anxious because I will need it for math class."

Positive "I message":
"When you wait for me after school, I feel glad because I won't have to wait for the bus alone."

Teamwork Part B

Look at the story below. How could you use what Mary said to Jesus to make a three-part "I message"?

Now every year his parents went to Jerusalem for the festival of the Passover. And when he was twelve years old, they went up as usual for the festival. When the festival was ended and they started to return, the boy Jesus stayed behind in Jerusalem, but his parents did not know it. Assuming that he was in the group of travelers, they went a day's journey. Then they started to look for him among their relatives and friends. When they did not find him, they returned to Jerusalem to search for him. After three days they found him in the temple, sitting among the teachers, listening to them and asking them questions. And all who heard him were amazed at his understanding and his answers. When his parents saw him they were astonished; and his mother said to him, "Child, why have you treated us like this? Look, your father and I have been searching for you in great anxiety." (Luke 2:41–48 NRSV)

Look at one or more of these "I messages" from God:

Isaiah 43:1–5
Jeremiah 29:10–14
Hebrews 13:5–6
1 Corinthians 10:13

Team Page *Straight Up* 24A

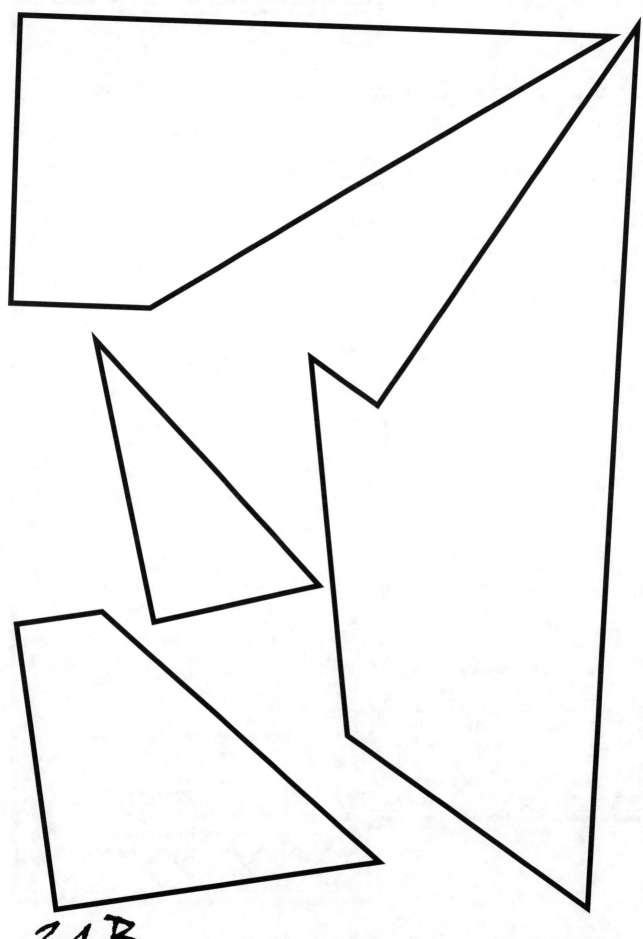

24B   **Team Page** *"T" Puzzle Cut-0uts*   © 1999 CPH

Get Real
Speaking with Authenticity

Introduction

Healthy communication requires honesty and authenticity. This session reinforces the "I message" skills practiced in lesson 24, which provide a framework for communicating thoughts, feelings, and needs accurately and without blaming.

Key Concept

Messages are authentic when youth speak honestly about their thoughts and feelings. The communication skill of using "I messages" also equips youth to better state their needs.

Goals

Youth will identify the "I message" format when communicating both positively and negatively, and recognize authentic responses to situations in life.

Bible Reference

1 Peter 1:22 NRSV

Lesson Overview

Activity	Summary	Goal	Materials	Time
Presession	Mural of things that make me mad	Casual group builder introducing theme	Newsprint or mural paper and marking pens, black plastic bags	Arrival/ Presession until class begins
Warm-up	Hit the target	Light-hearted fun focusing on anger points	Sponge	10 minutes
Focus	The three parts of an "I message"	Introduce the "I message" skill	Chalkboard and chalk or newsprint and marking pens	10 minutes
Activity	Hit the mark with an "I message"	Youth practice recognizing "I messages"	Team Page and pencils, situation cards from Teachers Guide	15 minutes
Bible Reflection	Messages from our heavenly Father	Read two passages from Scripture and respond to discussion	Team Page and pencils	10 minutes
Closing	Readings from the Bible and prayer	Refocus on the passages	Team Page	5 minutes

Presession: Things that Make Me Mad

Before youth arrive, tape a large piece of newsprint or mural paper with a black plastic bag behind it to the wall. Title it "Things that Make Me Mad." Give the youth marking pens and encourage them to draw pictures of things that get them angry. (Double thickness of paper or plastic garbage bags hung up behind the paper will help protect the wall.)

Warm-Up: Hit the Target

Have the group form a semicircle facing the "Things that Make Me Mad" mural. One at a time, each person in the line takes a damp sponge and throws it at the mural. The person who drew the drawing that is closest to where the sponge hits shares with the group what their drawing means. If the drawing has already been discussed, move to the next closest unshared item. Make sure everyone gets a chance to share.

Focus: "I Messages"

Say to the group, **There are lots of things that make us mad. We can submit, fight, or escape these problems, or we can assert ourselves and send an "I message." Today we are going to practice how to confront things that make us angry in a positive way.**

Use a chalkboard or newsprint and write a three-part "I message."

The three components of an "I message" include

- starting the message with the words "I feel ... ," then sharing the feeling.
- continuing "when ... ," describing the behavior without put-downs.
- concluding with "because ... ," which states the tangible effects the behavior has had upon you.

Example: "I feel _____ when _____ because _____."

Activity: Hit the "I Message" Target

This exercise works best in groups of four to six. Hand out the Team Page with pencils. Give each group a set of the photocopied cards from the "Situation Cards" page. (Make enough copies so that every four to six youth have a set.) Use Teamwork Part A to practice and evaluate "I messages" responding to the situations on the cards.

Bible Reflection: Team Page

Ask the youth to discuss the questions under Teamwork Part B. When they have talked about it for three to five minutes, ask the groups to share what they have discussed.

Closing

Read the two Bible passages from the Team Page aloud. Close with a prayer.

Your locker partner lets other kids use your locker, and it is so crowded that you can't find your stuff. This slows you up, and you have been late for class.

Your friend told someone that you have a crush on the new kid in class.

You arrive home late after a sports event, famished. Your mother had made your favorite meal, but there is nothing left of it.

Your teacher has explained a difficult assignment to you, but you still don't have a clue. When you ask for further instructions, the response is "You should understand by now."

You were sick and missed school. Your neighbor promised to bring the assignments but forgot. This could mean the difference between an A and a B.

You have been assigned a group science project. Most of the members share the work, but one person refuses to do his part. The project is due at the end of the week, and he hasn't done anything. You need his input to complete the assignment.

A friend told you she was busy and couldn't go to the mall with you. Then you found out she went to the movies with someone else.

You can't find your bike anywhere. You panic and look all over the neighborhood. You find it on the next block. Your sister took it to visit her friend.

A kid on the bus shoots spit wads at you. You change seats, yet he still does it.

You are eating M&M's and someone asks for some. When you pass the bag, they take them all.

You are waiting in a long line at the drinking fountain and three people cut in front of you.

Your parents are late picking you up at the mall, making you wait long after the time you had agreed to meet, even though they insisted you be on time.

For use with Team Page 25B.
Cut out these cards, making a set for every four to six participants.

Team Page *Situation Cards*

Teamwork Part A

Hit the bull's eye with a three-part "I message."

Get a set of cards from your teacher. Each person takes a card and reads the situation and tries to hit the "bull's eye" with a three-part "I message." The next person in line will be the judge of how accurate you were.

Record your score below.

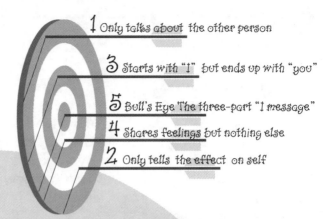

1 Only talks about the other person

3 Starts with "I" but ends up with "you"

5 Bull's Eye The three-part "I message"

4 Shares feelings but nothing else

2 Only tells the effect on self

"I message": When you _____ I feel _____ because _____.			
Names	**Round 1**	**Round 2**	**Round 3**
Totals			

Teamwork Part B

A Message from our Heavenly Father:

Where do selfish and hurtful words come from? (The sinful nature is incapable of doing genuine Christian good.)

How does faith in Christ Jesus change us and enable us to listen and speak better? (In Christ we are a new creation. See 2 Corinthians 5:17.)

What would your world be like if everyone followed the words of St. Peter that appear to the right?

How are we enabled to live as Peter and Paul recommend?

"Now that you have purified your souls by your obedience to the truth so that you have genuine mutual love, love one another deeply from the heart." (1 Peter 1:22 NRSV)

Jesus came to our world to bring harmony between God and people so there could be peace. How can you be assertive about your needs without putting down another person? "Let love be genuine; hate what is evil, hold fast to what is good." (Romans 12:9 NRSV)

Team Page *Get Real*

Win-Win Solutions
Problem Solving

Introduction
Youth are greatly affected by their relationships. In every relationship, conflicts happen. There are concrete steps to help resolve conflicts, improve relationships, and relieve stress.

Key Concept
Youth will identify six steps for discovering winning solutions.

Goals
Participants will learn some concrete steps for managing conflict.

Bible Reference
Joseph and his brothers (Genesis 45:1–18)

Presession: Dear Abby and Andy
Have youth write a short letter to a newspaper columnist about a conflict with friends or family. Collect and randomly exchange the letters. Ask the youth to write a "Dear Abby" or "Dear Andy" reply.

Warm-Up: All Knotted Up
Have youth stand in a circle, facing each other. Instruct them to extend their hands into the middle and join each of their hands with one hand of a different person (do not join with either of your neighbors; only two people to a link).

Lesson Overview

Activity	Summary	Goal	Materials	Time
Presession	Conflict news column	Be reminded of conflict situations	Paper, pencils	Arrival to beginning of session
Warm-up	A tangled group becomes a circle	Applying skills for knot solving to conflict resolution	Directions in Teachers Guide	10 minutes
Focus	Steps involved in conflict management	Teach basic principles	Teachers Guide and Team Page	15 minutes
Activity	Hypothetical situations in which steps are utilized	Youth will experience six steps through action	Teachers Guide	15 minutes
Bible Reflection	Discuss Joseph's options and choices	See Joseph as a model	Bible and Team Page	10 minutes
Closing	Use song for reflection	Youth express themselves in song	CD or tape of James Taylor's "You've Got a Friend"	5 minutes

This forms a knot of arms and hands. The challenge is to untangle the knot without losing hand contact, until students form a circle.

Focus: Let's Win This

In this session, youth are introduced to win-win solutions and six steps to get there. Begin by briefly reviewing the other possible solution styles: "I win, you lose," "You win, I lose," and "If I can't win, we both lose." Read a few of the Dear Abby and Andy letters from the Presession activity. Have students identify times when youth have been the "winners" and their friends or family have been the "losers." Discuss situations in which the youth have been "losers" and their friends or family have "won." Help them think about how they felt in each situation and what it did to their relationship with the other person.

Say, **Disagreements with others are bound to happen. Think about our Dear Abby and Andy letters. When conflict happens, sometimes someone has to give in. From the examples you cited or others you can think of, describe a situation in which you might be the "winner" and someone else might be the "loser."** Allow time for sharing. Focus on the feelings youth share. **Give examples when you lost and had to "give up" your needs in order to solve the situation.** Again, allow youth time to share. Focus on the feelings youth describe. **There are times when you have to follow the rules that those in authority have set over you. You have to comply. But there are other times when a little brainstorming might meet your needs and the needs of the others in the disagreement. Let's explore that model.**

Hand out the Team Page. **There are six helpful steps to finding a win-win solution when you have a problem or conflict.**

The first and most important step is to define both people's needs. Ask yourself what you really need (not want) in this situation. Precisely identify your needs, and also listen intently to what the other person needs. By actively listening, or parroting feedback, you can be sure to understand what they need. "I messages" are helpful.

Once you have identified the needs and expressed them to each other, step two involves brainstorming as many ways to solve this conflict as possible. Avoid judging any suggestions as stupid or dumb. Look for creative solutions together that neither one of you may have thought of before.

Step three is where you evaluate all the ideas you brainstormed. Try to remain as open-minded as possible. Discuss how each suggestion might work, or its drawbacks. Listen to each other and be determined to find a mutually satisfying solution.

The fourth step is to choose a solution. It may involve ranking or voting if the first choice is not clear. Try to shape the solution so that all parties are satisfied.

The fifth step involves implementing the solution so that each party can walk away knowing the clear details of how things will happen. Resolve any questions, and make the clarifications necessary.

The last step is to follow up, checking to see how the solution is working. Any problems should be addressed, and if the solution is not meeting the needs of someone involved, modify the plan. Repeat this sixth step of evaluation as often as necessary to ensure that the plan of action is working.

Activity: Summer Fun

Divide the class in two. Read the following scenario, and assign each group one of the sides. Using the model presented, have them solve the problem.

The middle school is deciding what year-end celebration activity to do. You all have been selected to serve on a committee that will decide whether to go to the local amusement park or to the beach. At the first meeting, the committee divides into two groups, each with definite opinions.

Bible Reflection: Team Page

In the story of Joseph's reunion with his brothers, both he and they had obvious needs. How did Joseph choose to solve everyone's needs? Was it a win-win solution? What could he have chosen to do instead?

What kind of solution was Jesus' life on earth? His death? His resurrection? How do we receive the benefits of a win-win solution with Him?

Closing: You've Got a Friend

Get a copy of the James Taylor song "You've Got a Friend." Have the youth listen or sing along. You might even lip-synch the words to a video camera.

Six Steps to Solving a Problem so Everyone Wins

(and you won't lose any friends)

1. **Clearly define and express each person's needs. Actively listen, parrot feedback, and use "I messages" in the process.**

2. **Brainstorm all possible ways to solve this problem. Don't judge any ideas as being stupid. Have fun and be silly.**

3. **Decide which possibilities will work or not work and why. Adapt and adjust them to find one that will work for both parties.**

4. **Agree on one solution that benefits both parties and is liveable.**

5. **Make a plan for carrying the solution out, and decide how it will work. Who will do what? How will they do it? When will they do it?**

6. **Later, periodically check back to make sure the plan is really being done. If it is not working, revise it and try again.**

Then Joseph could no longer control himself before all those who stood by him, and he cried out, "Send everyone away from me." So no one stayed with him when Joseph made himself known to his brothers. And he wept so loudly that the Egyptians heard it, and the household of Pharaoh heard it. Joseph said to his brothers, "I am Joseph. Is my father still alive?" But his brothers could not answer him, so dismayed were they at his presence. Then Joseph said to his brothers, "Come closer to me." And they came closer. He said, "I am your brother, Joseph, whom you sold into Egypt. And now do not be distressed, or angry with yourselves, because you sold me here; for God sent me before you to preserve life. For the famine has been in the land these two years; and there are five more years in which there will be neither plowing nor harvest. God sent me before you to preserve for you a remnant on earth, and to keep alive for you many survivors. So it was not you who sent me here, but God; he has made me a father to Pharaoh, and lord of all his house and ruler over all the land of Egypt. Hurry and go up to my father and say to him, 'Thus says your son Joseph, God has made me lord of all Egypt; come down to me, do not delay. You shall settle in the land of Goshen, and you shall be near me, you and your children and your children's children, as well as your flocks, your herds, and all that you have. I will provide for you there—since there are five more years of famine to come—so that you and your household, and all that you have, will not come to poverty.' And now your eyes and the eyes of my brother Benjamin see that it is my own mouth that speaks to you. You must tell my father how greatly I am honored in Egypt, and all that you have seen. Hurry and bring my father down here." Then he fell upon his brother Benjamin's neck and wept, while Benjamin wept upon his neck. And he kissed all his brothers and wept upon them; and after that his brothers talked with him. When the report was heard in Pharaoh's house, "Joseph's brothers have come," Pharaoh and his servants were pleased. Pharaoh said to Joseph, "Say to your brothers, 'Do this: load your animals and go back to the land of Canaan. Take your father and your households and come to me, so that I may give you the best of the land of Egypt, and you may enjoy the fat of the land.' " (Genesis 45:1–18 NRSV)

Bible Reflection

Read the Bible passages. How did Joseph handle his brothers? Why did he choose to do it that way?

What kind of solution was Jesus' life on earth? His death? His resurrection? How do we receive the benefits of a win-win solution with Him?

27 Put-Downs, Tear Downs

Introduction

When we put someone down we destroy their self-esteem. People naturally struggle with low self-esteem, which robs them of their full functions as people of God. In Christ we are affirmed and we can affirm others. Caring friends avoid put-downs.

Key Concept

Sin robs us of a healthy self-esteem. Christ gives us positive self-esteem. As He lives in us, He gives our lives meaning and purpose.

Goals

Participants will learn about the destructive nature of put-downs, the power of Christ to build up and affirm, and the value of shared, guided-prayer time.

Bible Reference

Scripture: Selected passages of affirmation

Presession

Distribute at least 30-40 vanilla wafers to each student or to groups of students. Instruct them to build a tower with them and to protect it from falling. Group members may not touch any other tower, but they may try to knock down another tower by blowing on it. Discuss, **Which is harder ... to build a tower or to keep it standing? How are these towers like our self-esteem? How and why do others try to knock them down? How do we protect our self-esteem?**

Lesson Overview

Activity	Summary	Goal	Materials	Time
Presession	Cookie towers	Students build towers with cookies	Vanilla wafers, 30–40 per person or group	Before class time
Warm-up	Brainstorm put-downs	Introduce theme and explore the experience	Paper plates, marking pens or crayons, chalkboard or newsprint	15 minutes
Activity	Plate Toss	Action simulation of tear-downs	Large playing area, decorated paper plates	15 minutes
Focus	Discuss the experience	Ask, "What did we learn?"	Team Page, pencils	5 minutes
Bible Reflection	Rebuilding the plates	See how Jesus builds us up	Large poster plate, masking tape, marking pens or crayons, Team Page	15 minutes
Closing	Guided imagery	Meditation	Teachers Guide	10 minutes

Warm-Up: Brainstorm

Have each youth draw a heart on a paper plate. Ask the class to share some examples of things people might say that hurt others' feelings. Summarize these comments on the chalkboard or newsprint, and instruct the youth to copy them around the outside of their heart.

Activity: Plate Toss

Because this activity may be loud and active, you may want to move outside or into a gymnasium. If neither of these are options, stay in class and be creative with the space.

Demonstrate how a paper plate can be used as a flying disk. With a partner, have one person throw and the other measure (in steps) how far their partner can throw the plate (in two tries).

Get everyone's attention and say, Remember your best distance. Tear off one of the put-down words along the edge outside the heart and throw it into the waste basket. Toss the plate again and measure it. Repeat this exercise until all the words are gone and only the heart remains.

Focus: Back in Teams

Gather the youth in groups of four to six. Distribute the Team Page and ask them to record their thoughts from the Plate Toss game in Teamwork Part A. Allow five minutes.

Bible Reflection: Rebuilding the Heart

Before class, create a large sample paper plate with poster board and marking pens. Draw a heart in the center of the plate.

In class, write these words around the heart: friend, branch, fruit, love, joy, and chosen.

Tear off each word and put a circle of masking tape on the back so the plate can be put back together.

In turn, ask each group to read one of the passages on Teamwork Part B. As each passage is read, have a volunteer place the appropriate piece back on the heart.

Respond to the questions on the Team Page.

Closing: Guided Prayer Time

Lead the class to prayer with a guided journey. Make certain that students close their eyes and remain quiet, so that they can listen to your voice as you lead them on the imaginary journey. Read the following with 10-second pauses between each phrase:

Imagine that you are walking outside on a warm spring day.

As you walk, you see Jesus coming toward you.

Because you somehow know it is He, you are not afraid.

He comes up to you and without saying a word, He looks deeply at you as if studying everything about you. He smiles a big smile and takes your hand.

As you walk with Him you notice another person coming into view. You know this person pretty well, but you do not get along with the person very well.

Jesus leads you up to the person and looks at this person, smiling the same way He smiled at you.

Then Jesus takes the other person's hand and the three of you walk. It is warm and sunny and you feel safe and secure.

Now Jesus stops. As He looks down at both of you, you know He wants you to hold hands with the other person too. Now the three of you are standing, holding hands, in a circle.

Now Jesus puts His hands on your shoulders and then, suddenly, He disappears, leaving you holding the hand of your new friend.

Now open your eyes, and hold the hand of the person next to you as we pray: Thank You, Jesus, for making us friends in You.

Teamwork Part A

From the plate toss game we learned:

_____

_____

_____

_____

Teamwork Part B

When people say harmful or hurtful things, remember that Jesus says, "I do not call you servants any longer, because the servant does not know what the master is doing; but I have called you friends" (John 15:15 NRSV).

"If the world hates you, be aware that it hated me before it hated you. ... I am the vine, you are the branches" (John 15:18, 5 NRSV).

"Those who abide in me and I in them bear much fruit, because apart from me you can do nothing" (John 15:5 NRSV).

"If you keep my commandments, you will abide in my love, just as I have kept my Father's commandments and abide in his love" (John 15:10 NRSV).

"I have said these things to you so that my joy may be in you, and that your joy may be complete" (John 15:11 NRSV).

"You did not choose me but I chose you. And I appointed you to go and bear fruit, fruit that will last. ... I am giving you these commands so that you may love one another" (John 15:16a, 17 NRSV).

What kinds of things might tear away at the heart of God? How might our words and actions tear away at God's love in our hearts? How does Jesus mend broken hearts? In what ways can the forgiveness of our sins also help us reach out to help and share the healing message with others?

What does it mean for you that Jesus says, "I have loved you with an everlasting love"?

Team Page *Put-Downs, Tear Downs*

I Am What I Am
Discovering Personality Styles

Introduction

During the early 1900s, Swiss psychiatrist Carl Jung recognized basic differences in human personalities. Many others have built upon his work to help us understand that people have different ways of perceiving, interpreting, and responding to the world. This awareness can help us better understand motivation and behavior. It can expand our tolerance and respect for those who are different from us. By understanding these differences, we are less likely to think that we are right and others are wrong, helping us to become better caring friends.

Key Concept

God made each person unique. This session will help students appreciate their own unique characteristics and begin to develop an appreciation for others.

Bible Reference

The styles of Peter, John, Martha, Esther

Goals

Each participant will learn about the four main personality styles of the inventory: Friendship, Action, Imagination, and Reflection. They will choose a preference and try to discover the personalities of four biblical characters.

Lesson Overview

Activity	Summary	Goal	Materials	Time
Presession	Matching famous people to personality types	Developing the concept that people are different	Old magazines, scissors, glue, four poster boards	Arrival/Presession
Warm-up	You-nique	Sentence stems that describe individuals	Team Page, pencils	15 minutes
Focus	Introduction to styles	Prepare students to take a personality analysis	Teachers Guide	10 minutes
Activity	The Personality Style Inventory	Help students understand more about their personality	Team Page, pencils	30 minutes
Bible Reflection	Bible heroes are of different types	Show how God made people of all styles	Team Page, pencils	15 minutes

Presession: Famous Types

Prepare a separate poster board for each of these words: Friendship, Action, Imagination, and Reflection. As youth arrive, have them cut out pictures of famous people from magazines and glue them to the poster that best describes their personality.

Warm-Up: You-nique

Hand out the Bonus Team Pages 1A and 1B and pencils. Ask students to complete the six sentence stems in Teamwork Part A. When finished, have them find everyone else with the same or a similar answer for the first sentence stem, and then stand in a group. Point out the strengths of clusters and of individuality.

Focus: Name It

God has made each of you a unique individual. When you know who you are, you appreciate God's work and give Him praise. We know that people do not all look, talk, or act the same. Neither do people think or learn in the same way. Some people gather information by watching and reflecting. Some people learn best when they can try and do things that are active. You can like who you are.

People also process information differently. Some people think about information, and others use their feelings to make sense of information. One way is not better than the other. They are just different. We will see that some Bible characters were very different from each other, yet they each accomplished important things for God.

Activity: Personality Style Inventory

Have students follow the instructions for Teamwork Part B, circling one word in each row that best describes them. After everyone has completed all 15 items, have them total the circles in each column and enter the number in the box at the bottom of that column. The largest number of circles may be their preferred type.

F = Friendship R = Reflection A = Action I = Imagination. Read the descriptions from the back of the Team Page. If students wonder about their score, allow them to look over the items again and make any changes that are necessary. Point out that a tie may be a good thing, showing a balance between different styles. People tend to use their second style in times of stress or conflict.

Bible Reflection: Team Page

Form groups of youth with an even distribution of "types" in each. Ask them to read the passages about Peter, Martha, John, and Esther in Teamwork Part C. After the groups have looked at each Bible character, have them decide which personality type best describes each character. If time is short, assign one biblical character to each group and have them share their discovery with the large group.

Peter is Imagination.
Martha is Action.
John is Friendship.
Esther is Reflection.

Other Resources

Please Understand Me: Character and Temperament Types by David Keirsey and Marilyn Bates. Distributed by Prometheus Nemesis Book Company, Box 2082, Del Mar, California 92014. Phone: (619) 632-1575

Teamwork Part A *Complete the following sentences:*

1   My favorite pastime is … _____

2   My best subject in school is … _____

3   My favorite restaurant is … _____

4   My favorite TV show is … _____

5   One thing I often pray for is … _____

6   My favorite Bible story is … _____

Teamwork Part B *Personality Style Inventory*

Directions

Please circle the word that best describes you from each number below.

1. understanding	accuracy	realism	imagination
2. cooperate	thought provoking	active	excited
3. listen and share	reflect	experiment	explore a hunch
4. harmony	precise	efficient	adventurous
5. caring	correctness	determined	intuitive
6. sensitive	critical	completion	impulsive
7. cooperative	orderly	straightforward	free-spirit
8. sociable	inquisitive	high standards	relaxed
9. personal value	reasoning	common sense	flexible
10. hesitant	consistent	aggressive	disorganized
☐ **F**	☐ **R**	☐ **A**	☐ **I**

Friendly Personality

- This person needs cooperation, personal security, and acceptance.
- You are uncomfortable with conflict.
- You value personal relationships, helping others, and being liked. Thus, you will sacrifice your own likes or desires in order to win approval from others.
- You prefer to work with other people in a team effort rather than individually.
- You are friendly, supportive, respectful, willing, dependable, and agreeable.
- You are people-oriented.

Reflective Personality

- You are most concerned with being organized, having all the facts, and being careful before taking action.
- Your need is to be accurate and to be right.
- You are precise and orderly and follow organizational rules and historical ways of doing things.
- You are task-oriented.
- You use facts and data.
- You are comfortable in positions in which you can check facts and figures and be sure you are right.

Team Page *I Am What I Am* **1A**
Bonus

Active Personality

- You are action- and goal-oriented.
- You need to accomplish things and see results.
- You have a quick reaction time and are decisive, independent, disciplined, practical, and efficient.
- You use facts and data.
- You tend to speak and act quickly.
- You are comfortable in positions of leadership.

Imaginative Personality

- You enjoy involvement, excitement, and interpersonal action. You are sociable, stimulating, enthusiastic, and are good at involving and motivating others.
- You are idea-oriented.
- You have less concern for routine and are future-oriented.
- You have a quick reaction time.
- You have a need to be accepted by others.
- You tend to be spontaneous, outgoing, energetic, and friendly.
- You are focused on people rather than on tasks.
- You use opinions and stories rather than facts and data.

Each personality is different—and important!

Teamwork Part C

Decide which of the above personality styles best describes the biblical characters described in the following verses: Peter, Martha, John, Esther.

I think Peter may have had a _____ personality.
John 21:1–22

I think Martha may have had a _____ personality.
Luke 10:38–42

I think John may have had a _____ personality.
John 19:26–27

I think Esther may have had a _____ personality.
Esther 4

How does God's love for these four different individuals give you assurance about His love for you? Does our personality make a difference on how forgiven we are or how important we are to God? How might it shape the way God blesses us? How might it affect our life in eternity?

**1B
Bonus**

Team Page *I Am What I Am*

Listen, Listen
Measuring Your Listening Style

Bonus

Introduction

This is a test of a caring friend's listening skills. Since people listen differently, this session will help caring friends discover their listening style and consider adapting their style to become a more effective listener.

Goals

Participants will discover their listening style and consider other styles that may be more effective when helping a friend. Because the Team Page may take a while to complete, you will only have time for the Warm-up, the Activity, and a Closing.

Warm-Up: Listen Up!

Distribute paper and pencils. Ask participants to list their favorite food, sport, and TV show. Gather in a large circle and have each person share their name and their three answers. For example, I might say, "Kurt, pizza, football, *The Simpsons*." After everyone has shared, ask them to try writing down one thing they remember from each person's list. Let them share how well they listened. Award a small prize to the person(s) who remember them all.

Lesson Overview

Activity	Summary	Goal	Materials	Time
Warm-up	Listening game	Learn names and begin thinking about listening skills	Blank paper, pencils	15 minutes
Activity	Listening profile	Help youth value different listening styles	Teachers Guide, Team Page, pencils	30 minutes
Closing	1 John 4:7–12	Love is of God	Teachers Guide or Bible	5 minutes

Activity: Your Listening Style

Distribute the Team Page and pencils. Ask the youth to listen to each statement and choose a response from the list. Have them work alone quietly. Read the following statements with the appropriate emotion and inflection. Pause as the youth choose their response.

Statements

1. Boy—age 13

"This year I'm going to get good grades. I'm not afraid of hard work. I'll do whatever it takes because my future depends on great grades. I need to attend the best college possible. I want to be somebody."

2. Girl—age 16

"That Jamie Jones is so smart. She makes me so mad! She thinks she knows all the answers. She thinks she's going to be the valedictorian. I'll show her. I am going to work harder and get even better grades, easily!"

3. Girl—age 15

"We've lived here for five years now. I've been going to this same school for two years, but I still don't have any really good friends. I just freeze up. I try to be easy-going, but I just feel all stiff and uncomfortable inside. Sometimes I try to tell myself that I don't really care. Everybody's just out for themselves—you can't count on most kids anyway. Sometimes I really believe that I don't honestly want any friends."

4. Boy—age 13

"The coach suggested that I give up trying to be a point guard and shift over to tryouts for forwards. He thinks I've got a pretty good chance to make the team because I'm big and aggressive, but he gave me the choice. Being a forward is not as spectacular as what I wanted, but I'm not sure I'd be the best ball handler. I'd rather play regularly than warm the bench. I'm ready to give up the flashy stuff just to be on the team."

Ask the students to turn over the Team Page and score their responses. Help the youth to discover their style. Discuss how an understanding response can keep the conversation moving, focused on the speaker.

Closing

Gather back in a circle and announce, **Each person here is important. If any one of you were missing today, it would have been a different experience. Listen to these words from 1 John, chapter 4: "Beloved, let us love one another, because love is from God; everyone who loves is born of God and knows God. Whoever does not love does not know God, for God is love. God's love was revealed among us in this way: God sent his only Son into the world so that we might live through him. In this is love, not that we loved God but that he loved us and sent his Son to be the atoning sacrifice for our sins. Beloved, since God loved us so much, we also ought to love one another. No one has ever seen God; if we love one another, God lives in us, and his love is perfected in us." (1 John 4:7–12 NRSV)**

How do you think God is as a listener? Why? How does it feel to know that He always listens? What does it mean for us when we need to talk to somebody about really important stuff? How is Jesus' death on the cross a kind of "listening" to our sins and the perfect response to our need? What is Jesus' response?

Developing Listening Skills

Listen to the different speakers as your teacher reads, then mark the one choice that would be your typical response.

A

1. You think of yourself as ambitious, is that it?
2. You feel that you have to be on top no matter what.
3. Sounds like you really have a strong need to get ahead.
4. Would you like to see a video I have on how to study to get A's? It could help you.
5. Good grades are a good thing, but are you really sure you want to work that hard? You might miss out on other fun things.

B

1. It sounds like it is really important that you do better then she does.
2. It's okay to want to do your best, but do you really think your attitude about her is right?
3. It will take a lot of hard study to be valedictorian. You'll really need to plan your work and keep your schedule free to study. Are you sure you want that?
4. She really makes you want to beat her, doesn't she?
5. Hold on a minute here ... why do you want to beat her?

C

1. Here is what we can do. Why don't you come along to youth group at our church? It's a great place to make friends. What do you think?
2. So what do you do when you want to make friends? Perhaps I could give you some suggestions, if I knew what you'd been doing already.
3. It sounds like you've waited a long time for it to get better, and it never does. I hear some frustration ... is that right?
4. Maybe you don't really want friends.
5. That's really sad. You need to learn how to make friends ... the sooner, the better.

D

1. It sounds like you've thought this through and really made a good choice. By going out for the forward position, you can build from there.
2. That sounds good to me. If you need any help learning the position, I'll work out with you.
3. So have you checked to see how many other guys are out for the forward position? Have you considered how tough that position might be?
4. Of course! Being point guard may be appealing, but your choice shows more maturity.
5. It may not be as spectacular to play forward, but it sounds like you really want to play more.

Your Listening Style

The letters A-D represent each statement. Circle the number of your response for each statement. Total up your circles, and check the descriptions below for your listening style.

Statements	Judge	Doctor	Rescuer	Investigator	Counselor
A	5	2	4	3	1
B	2	1	3	5	4
C	5	4	1	2	3
D	1	4	2	3	5
Total Circles					

Listening Skills

The key to listening is in your response. Most listening responses fall into one of five categories. These five types of responses are

The Judge: Makes a judgment based on what they think is right.

The Doctor: Tries to figure out what's wrong and makes some guesses about your thoughts, feelings, or motivations.

The Rescuer: Attempts to solve your problem or take care of you.

The Investigator: Attempts to gain more information.

The Counselor: Attempts to reflect back what you are saying, listening to what you are thinking and feeling.

3
Bonus

What Is Your Gift?
Multiple Intelligences

Intelligence Report

Have students page through magazines and find the picture of the person they feel is most intelligent. Share in the group. Have them go through again and find someone who is gifted at 1) thoughtfulness and reflection, philosophy; 2) people skills; 3) music; 4) use of the body; 5) art; 6) logic and math skills; 7) written expression. Discuss which one they admire most.

Have students fill out the Multiple Intelligences survey on the Bonus Team Pages 3A and 3B. Then have them break into groups to discuss the Bible Reflection questions.

Multiple Intelligences (Check any statements that apply to you.)

Intrapersonal Intelligence

- [ ] I spend time alone thinking about important stuff.
- [ ] I have opinions that set me apart from the crowd.
- [ ] I have a special hobby I like to do alone.
- [ ] I have some important goals for my life that I think about a lot.
- [ ] I consider myself to be an independent thinker.
- [ ] I keep a personal diary to record my thoughts and feelings about my life.

Interpersonal Intelligence

- [ ] People in school and the neighborhood come to me for advice.
- [ ] I prefer group sports like volleyball or softball rather than solo sports like track or swimming.
- [ ] I favor group pastimes such as board and card games over individual games like solitaire.
- [ ] I enjoy the challenge of telling others what I've learned.
- [ ] I consider myself a leader.
- [ ] I like to get involved in social activities connected with my school, church, or community.

Musical and Rhythmic Intelligence

- [ ] I have a pleasant singing voice.
- [ ] I play a musical instrument.
- [ ] My life would be sad if there were no music in it.
- [ ] I can easily keep time to some music by tapping my feet.
- [ ] I know the tunes to many different songs.
- [ ] If I hear music once or twice, I am usually able to sing it back fairly accurately.

Body and Kinesthetic Intelligence

- [ ] I engage in at least one sport or physical activity on a regular basis.
- [ ] I like using my hands for activities like carpentry, model-building, sewing, carving, or weaving.
- [ ] I like to spend my free time outdoors.
- [ ] I enjoy amusement rides or other thrilling physical experiences.
- [ ] I would describe myself as well-coordinated.
- [ ] I need to practice a skill rather than just read about it or see a video that describes it.

Visual and Spatial Intelligence

- [ ] I often see clear visual images when I close my eyes.
- [ ] I am sensitive to color.
- [ ] I enjoy doing jigsaw puzzles, mazes, and other visual puzzles.
- [ ] I like to draw or doodle.
- [ ] I can comfortably imagine how something might appear from a bird's-eye view.
- [ ] I prefer reading material with lots of illustrations.

Logical and Mathematical Intelligence

- [ ] I can easily compute numbers in my head.
- [ ] Math and science are my favorite subjects in school.
- [ ] I enjoy playing games or solving brain-teasers that require logical thinking.
- [ ] My mind searches for regular, logical sequences and patterns.
- [ ] I'm interested in new developments in the sciences.
- [ ] I believe that almost everything has a logical explanation.

Verbal and Linguistic Intelligence

- [ ] Books are very important to me.
- [ ] I can hear the words in my head before I speak or write them down.
- [ ] I am good at crossword puzzles and word games like Scrabble.
- [ ] I enjoy entertaining myself with tongue twisters, nonsense rhymes, and puns.
- [ ] English, social studies, and history are easier than math or science.
- [ ] I've written something recently that I was proud of or that earned recognition from others.

In which area did you have the most checks?

Team Page *What Is Your Gift?* **3A** **Bonus**

Multiple Intelligences

Most people have one or two intelligences that are stronger and more fully developed then the rest. Everyone has the capacity for nurturing all seven.

Intelligence	Descriptions	Strategies	Careers
Intrapersonal Intelligence	Intelligence of the inner self, intuition, and emotions	Using learning centers, participating in self-reflection tasks, using higher-order reasoning	Psychiatrists, counselors, entrepreneurs
Interpersonal Intelligence	Intelligence of people—relationship skills, communication skills, and collaborative skills	Working with mentors and tutors, participating in interactive projects, using cooperative learning	Teachers, politicians, religious leaders
Musical and Rhythmic Intelligence	Intelligence of recognition and use of rhythmic or tonal patterns and sensitivity to sounds	Singing, performing, writing compositions, playing instruments, performing choral readings	Musicians, advertising designers, composers
Body and Kinesthetic Intelligence	Intelligence of physical self, control of one's body movements, and learning by doing	Role playing, dancing, playing games, using manipulatives	Athletes, inventors, mechanics
Visual and Spatial Intelligence	Intelligence for pictures, mental images, and sight	Drawing, using guided imagery, making mind-maps, making charts	Architects, mechanical engineers, map makers
Logical and Mathematical Intelligence	Intelligence of numbers, logic, and inductive reasoning	Developing outlines, creating codes, calculating, problem solving	Accountants, lawyers, computer programmers
Verbal and Linguistic Intelligence	Intelligence of words and production of language	Journal writing, speech-making, storytelling, reading	Novelists, comedians, journalists

Based upon *Frames of Mind* (1983) by Howard Gardner

Bible Reflection

What does it mean that "I believe that God has made me …"? Did He make you the way you are? Does He love us because of our intelligence and how we use it? What does Romans 5:6–8 share about His love? Read Hebrews 11. Which intelligences are in this list? How can He use each one (including yours) for His work?

3B Bonus   **Team Page** *What Is Your Gift?*

Training Review of
Lasting Friendship Skills

NAME_____

Answer the following questions in either true/false or multiple choice fashion.

1. When you think of making friends, which of the following choices best describes this course, based on your experience?

   This course
   A. Is one way God has met my friendship needs.
   B. Has helped my relationships with others and improved my popularity.
   C. Taught me how Christ is reflected in my relationships with others.
   D. Taught me that my relationships with others are based on simple communication techniques.

2. Being a friend to someone means becoming their best friend.
   True   False

3. Being a friend to someone means being available to help.
   True   False

4. One of the best ways to help others with their friendships is to
   A. Listen to them.
   B. Distract them so they think of something other than their problems.
   C. Give advice on what they should do.

5. Knowing that every person is a special creation of God, which of the following is true?
   A. Knowing how others "tick" can really give me insight on making friends.
   B. Knowing how I am unique will help me relate to others like me.
   C. Knowing myself helps me understand differences and how to work through them.

6. God has a purpose for each of us while we are here on earth, and it is our job to discover what that purpose is.
   True   False

7. Knowing your personality style can
   A. Allow you deeper understanding and appreciation of people in general.
   B. Give you an advantage when arguing with someone.
   C. Help you better understand your relationships with others.
   D. All of the above

8. According to the brief descriptions of the four personality styles, which style is most like you?
   A. Friendship
   B. Reflection
   C. Action
   D. Imagination

9. Two types of questions that can really open up a discussion are
   A. Closed and open.
   B. Closed and feelings level.
   C. Open and feelings level.
   D. Open and judgmental.

10. Identify which of the following questions/statements are closed (C), open (O), feelings level (F), or informational (I). There may be more than one category.
    _____What time are you going to the game?
    _____What was that like?
    _____You look angry. What happened?
    _____Why did you do it that way?
    _____I would like to know why you did it that way so I can understand.
    _____Do you throw things when you get mad?

Learning Exercise 4A
Bonus

_____What do you do when you are angry?

_____You look embarrassed. Can you tell me why?

_____What do you want for Christmas?

11. We communicate most of our messages to others through
   A. What we say.
   B. Our nonverbal communication.

12. It is important to pay attention to someone. Some of the ways we show our attention are called "attending behaviors." Identify which of these attending behaviors are effective (E) and which are ineffective (I).
   _____Looking into another's eyes
   _____Leaning toward the speaker if you are seated
   _____Smiling
   _____Tapping your fingers
   _____Crossing your arms
   _____Holding your finger to your lips
   _____Speaking in a soft voice
   _____Talking with a fast rate of speech

13. Empathy means
   A. To be able to "walk in another's shoes."
   B. Letting bygones be bygones.
   C. Not to let things "get to you."
   D. To not allow the sun to set on your anger.

14. Paraphrasing and parroting help the person to feel
   A. Helpful.
   B. Important.
   C. Listened to and understood.
   D. Like they influence you and others.

15. Focusing on feelings is something most of us do not even consider when communicating with others.
   True   False

Choose a listening/feeling response to the following situations:

16a. Sue has just been dumped by her boyfriend.
   A. Did he say why he dumped you?
   B. There are more fish in the sea.
   C. You're really feeling that he is a jerk.
   D. Sounds like you're feeling let down.

16b. Your friend just got caught cheating.
   A. Wow! That must have been embarrassing.
   B. You dummy—did you think he wouldn't notice?
   C. Did the kids in the room laugh at you?
   D. Next time you should try this instead …

16c. Your friend was just notified about being one credit short of graduating. Your response is
   A. I can't believe Mrs. Brown didn't catch that!!
   B. Well, then just go to night school.
   C. What did you fail that made you a credit short?
   D. You look down. What's going on?

17. When you are genuine, you speak for yourself and try not to be judgmental. What are the components of a good "I message"?
   A. When you _____ because _____ I need_____.
   B. When you _____ I feel _____ _____ because _____.
   C. I need _____ because _____ if not, then _____ so _____.
   D. I feel _____ when you _____ if not, then _____ because _____.

4B
Bonus
Learning Exercise

Check the best "I message" from the following:

18a. Your friend is late, forcing you to change big plans.
   A. Great! Now we get to do something stupid instead!!
   B. I'm so mad!! You could have called or something!!
   C. I'm so upset that you are 45 minutes late. What a jerk!!
   D. I'm upset that you're late because now we have to change plans. I need you to be on time.

18b. Your parents keep bugging you about keeping your room clean. It is hard to do because you share the room with your brother or sister.
   A. Mom, you really don't understand how hard this is to keep clean with him/her here!
   B. I'm so frustrated when you yell at me about this room because I'm not the one who messes it up.
   C. This is so unfair! You never yell at him/her, just me!
   D. It is really annoying to get yelled at about this room. Why don't you try yelling at him/her too?

18c. A friend has been avoiding you for the last few days and you don't know why.
   A. I feel that you are neglecting me when you don't talk to me. What is going on?
   B. I don't like to be ignored. What is the problem?
   C. You must really be mad at me. What do you want me to do?
   D. I feel left out when you don't talk to me because I worry that I did something wrong. What's going on?

19. Assertive communication includes
   A. Giving in to requests from others.
   B. Using blame and sarcasm.
   C. Feeling guilty about saying no.
   D. Standing up for one's legitimate rights.

Read James 1:19–27. What hints does this passage contain for being a caring friend? How was Jesus the best friend who ever lived? Can you think of any times that He listened to people without judging? Can you think of any times that He spoke things that were comforting to them? Can you think of any times when He accepted people for their unique personalities? Because Jesus is the perfect friend, He is able to help make us better at friendship skills.

Learning Exercise 4C
Bonus

Practice Session Ideas

Listening for Feelings

Listening for feelings seems quite easy. Yet it is difficult to remember to use this helpful listening skill. This activity can be used any time review is needed.

Speaker: I hate school!

Listener: You are not happy with school?

The speaker has lots of feelings and expresses them with words.

The listener tries to understand the speaker's feelings by asking what he thinks she is feeling.

Practice listening to each other.

Step one: Find a partner.

Step two: Flip a coin to decide who will speak and who will listen.

Step three: The speaker shares something important going on in their life. The listener tries to guess the feeling. (Go for three minutes.)

Step four: The speaker give some feedback to the listener on how well they listened.

Last step: Switch roles and follow steps three and four.

Gospel Bonus

Caring friends do not preach to their friends, but it is helpful to know some words of Scripture to use when talking with someone who is struggling with something in their life.

Distribute the student sheet. Have students work individually or in small groups, using the concordance in the back of the Bible to find at least one Bible passage to use for each category. Encourage students to keep this card handy.

Write down at least one Bible reference that might be helpful in each of these situations. Use the concordance.

1 When lonely

2 When struggling with temptation

3 When rejected by friends

4 After committing a grave sin

5 When struggling to make a decision

6 When it is time to make a decision

7 When under stress

8 When having doubts about God

9 After a fight with someone

10 When someone has died

11 When life is too busy

12 When you've lost something or someone

13 When something is missing from life

14 When discouraged

15 When disappointed

Appendix: Resources for Teachers

All Lessons:

Skills for Living: Group Counseling Activities for Young Adolescents
by Rosemarie Smead Morganett
Research Press, 2612 North Mattis Avenue, Champaign, Illinois 61821
ISBN: 0-87822-318-5

Do It! Active Learning in Youth Ministry
by Thom and Joani Schultz
Group Books, Box 481, Loveland, Colorado 89539
ISBN: 0-93152-994-8

A Junior High Kinda Guy (video)
Pat Hurley
A three-tape package covering a wide range of topics including peer pressure, biblical self-esteem, parent relationships, academic excellence, how to deal with failure, and high dating standards.
Part 1 Relationship series
Part 2 Issues series
Part 3 Self-Esteem series

What Kids Need to Succeed: Proven, Practical Ways to Raise Good Kids
by Peter L. Benson, Judy Galbraith, and Pamela Espeland
Free Spirit Publishing Inc., 4000 First Avenue North, Suite 616, Minneapolis, Minnesota 55401-1730.
ISBN: 1-57542-030-9

Lesson 6:

"Standing Outside the Fire" (song) by Garth Brooks
Hidden Carefully: Facing the Problems of Alcoholism (video) International Lutheran Women's Missionary League, running time 26 minutes

Lesson 7:

There is a great story that could augment this lesson or perhaps replace the Buckets story. It is the story of the Wemicks on page 51 of *Tell Me the Secrets* by Max Lucado, illustrated by Ron DiCianni. It is available in many Christian bookstores. It is published by Crossway Books, Wheaton, Illinois.
ISBN: 0-80107-730-8

Lesson 9:

White Rock Blues (video) Ray Cioni
This discussion starter is an animated fantasy giving important clues to discovering who you are and why you are here.

Lesson 11:

Old Turtle by Douglas Wood, illustrated by Cheng-Khee Chee.
Pfeifer Hamilton Publisher, 210 West Michigan, Duluth MN 55802.
ISBN: 0-93858-648-3

Lesson 16:

Music Box (video)
Follow the changing feelings of the main character. Award-winning allegorical drama of a factory worker who, after finding a music box, discovers "hallelujah" in his "ho-hum" life.
White Lion Media. Running time 20 minutes.

Lesson 19:

"Blind Man" (song) by Lost and Found. Available from them at P.O. Box 142, Maumee, Ohio 43537. (419) 897-9792. HENGH@aol.com

Bonus Lesson 1:

Please Understand Me: Character and Temperament Types
by David Keirsey and Marilyn Bates
Prometheus Nemesis Book Company, Box 2082, Del Mar, California 92014
ISBN: 0-96069-540-0